Lucian Müller, Samuel Ball Platner

Greek and Roman Versification

With an Introduction on the Development of Ancient Versification

Lucian Müller, Samuel Ball Platner

Greek and Roman Versification
With an Introduction on the Development of Ancient Versification

ISBN/EAN: 9783744776721

Printed in Europe, USA, Canada, Australia, Japan

Cover: Foto ©ninafisch / pixelio.de

More available books at **www.hansebooks.com**

WITH

*AN INTRODUCTION ON THE DEVELOPMENT
OF ANCIENT VERSIFICATION*

BY

LUCIAN MÜLLER

TRANSLATED BY

SAMUEL BALL PLATNER
Professor in Adelbert College

Boston
ALLYN AND BACON
1892

TRANSLATOR'S NOTE.

Lucian Müller's "Metrik der Griechen und Römer" (2d ed., Leipzig, 1885) has met with so favorable a reception in Europe, and is in so many respects a valuable handbook, that it has seemed to be worth while to translate it into English, with the author's sanction.

Almost all students in our preparatory schools and colleges are sadly deficient in their knowledge of Latin and Greek versification, and any help whatever towards remedying this condition of things may not be amiss. Hence this translation, in which no changes have been introduced except the musical notation.

S. B. P.

July, 1892.

PREFACE TO THE SECOND EDITION.

THE kind reception of this book, which was published in the beginning of 1880 in Russian, and has already been most carefully translated into French and Italian, of necessity spurred me on to make it still better adapted to subserve its intended purpose. Hence the criticisms, offered in the different reviews of the book, as in the "Philologische Rundschau" (1881, No. 38) and the "Revue Critique" (1881, Nos. 36 and 52), have been conscientiously considered and, as far as possible, made use of. I am especially indebted to Professor A. Eussner, who has called my attention to various inequalities in the work. The addition of an Alphabetical Index to this edition, as well as to the French and Italian translations, will please many readers.

I have not succeeded in accomplishing the desire, several times expressed, to treat exhaustively of the metres of Catullus in this little book. For these I must refer to the "Summarium rei metricæ poetarum latinorum," St. Petersburg and Leipzig, 1878, a work which has retained its popularity even by the side of the German 'Metrik,' as is shown by the continuous demand for it.

L. M.

ST. PETERSBURG, January 1, 1885.

PREFACE TO THE FIRST EDITION.

The thought which has influenced me most in the composition of this book, is that which I have already expressed on page 101 of my Biography of Ritschl, namely, that a knowledge of the most usual classical metres, founded on a developed linguistic sense, is the most important and, in practice, the most necessary requirement — as well for the teacher as for the pupil in the gymnasium. Even among philologists there are few specialists in versification. How can more be asked of the students than is demanded above?

It is, however, a matter of great moment that this knowledge should not be simply mechanical, a mere exercise of the memory, but that it should be thoroughly understood and felt by the students, so that they, to speak with Horace, not only *legitimum sonum digitis callent*, but, as is most important, *aure*. Encouraged by the approval which has been bestowed in Germany, France, Russia, and elsewhere, upon my "Summary of Latin Versification," — a book intended, as is stated in the Preface, for students, teachers, and philologists, who are not specialists in this line, — and by its wide circulation, in spite of the fact that it is written in Latin, I now have decided to write a treatise on the versification of the Greeks and Romans, especially adapted for the upper classes in the gymnasia. To this task I have been repeatedly urged by highly esteemed teachers.

The method is exactly the same as that pursued in the "De re metrica poetarum latinorum." Following the examples of Hermann and Lachmann, and still more that of Bentley and Porson, the attempt is everywhere made to explain the phenomena of versification from a linguistic point of view. While there may be a difference of opinion concerning the scientific justification of this mode of procedure, a question that I have discussed at more length in the Biography of Ritschl, page 100, there can hardly be any doubt among intelligent teachers of its practical usefulness for the purpose of this handbook.

The great majority of judges who are qualified to express an opinion on the subject now acknowledge that grammatical accent is wholly without influence so far as the rhythmical formation of the classical metres is concerned. My own theory, which goes much further and amounts to this, that the main object of the old poets was to produce as great variation as possible between the poetical rhythm and the grammatical accent, and that in general, in the structure of the verse, no regard was had for the accent, but only for the number of syllables, especially for the balancing of monosyllables and polysyllables, still encounters much opposition. My only hope is that after reading the Fifth Section, even my most stubborn opponents will acknowledge that this view can be put to excellent use in actual practice.

In accordance with the object of this work the Greeks principally considered are Homer, the fragments of the Elegiac, Iambic, and Æolic poets, as far as they serve to illustrate Homer; among the tragedians, especially Sophocles; of the Romans, Vergil, Horace, Ovid, Phædrus, Tibullus, and Propertius. Only occasional references are made to the chorus and in general to the lyrical parts of the Greek tragedies, for the following reasons: —

In the first place, the criticism and metrical reconstruction of these parts is very uncertain, just as in the *cantica* of Plautus. Besides, a metrical scheme of these passages is found in all the editions ordinarily used; and although I have grave doubts about the accepted divisions, still any change in them would be dangerous without a longer argument, and polemical arguments would expand this book beyond its proper limits. Further, I am of the opinion that the teacher should read metrically the lyrical parts of tragedy, and require the same of the students, without lingering too long over the versification. Every teacher will admit that in the reading of a Greek drama in the gymnasia so many other difficult questions must be considered, that only a small portion of time can be given to metrical questions, if the reading of any particular play is to be finished or even carried to any considerable length. It is the object of the gymnasium to develop the understanding and imagination of the scholars, and to inspire in them a love and appreciation of classical antiquity, but not to make of them philologists or specialists in metre. Therefore I believe that I shall have fulfilled my duty if I succeed in bringing the students to know and understand the ordinary metres of those poets usually read in the gymnasia.

I have therefore treated especially of the two most frequent and noble metres, the Dactylic Hexameter and Iambic Trimeter (together with the Strophes of Horace), with the conviction that one who has thoroughly mastered these measures has already advanced a long way into the knowledge of ancient versification.

Just because versification is so often unreasonably neglected, a great part of the charm that poetry afforded to the men of olden time is veiled or wholly taken away from students. Every teacher knows that for most students, until they reach the highest classes in the gymnasium, scanning is a veritable "*crux*," which has contributed not a little to keep alive the prejudice against classical authors, while in reality the most beautiful creation of the genius of language is the versification of the classic poets which are read in the schools. To produce a love for this versification and an understanding of it, which may outlive the years of school life, is the purpose of this book.

Truly, I must beg for it an indulgent reception.

It is not easy in a handbook, which should be at once thoroughly scientific, brief, and generally intelligible, to satisfy all fair demands, not to mention the unfair. The task was all the harder because, although for a long time I have had a lively interest in the practical questions of classical philology as well as in the needs of the gymnasia, still on account of my position I have come but little into direct touch with these institutions, and so have been deprived of the equally inspiring and manifold impressions produced by daily immediate contact with youth. So much the more grateful ought I to be, that experienced teachers of different countries have assisted me with their advice. They were also, almost without exception, of the opinion that I should treat in only a cursory way of the lyrical parts of the Greek tragedy.

For the rest, perhaps this handbook, though primarily intended for the upper classes in the gymnasia, may prove not unwelcome to many students of philology, even the younger.

The introduction is, of course, principally for teachers and philologists. For the part treating of Greek versification I must ask indulgence, since in the metrical works known to me, even in the excellent book of Christ which I have often used, there is no simple connected statement of the development of Greek versification. For this part, as well as for the whole book, any corrections or hints of qualified philologists or teachers will be most welcome.

L. M.

St. Petersburg, January 1, 1880.

CONTENTS.

	PAGE
TRANSLATOR'S NOTE	3
PREFACE TO THE SECOND EDITION	4
PREFACE TO THE FIRST EDITION	5

INTRODUCTION.

DEVELOPMENT OF CLASSICAL VERSIFICATION.

1. General Remarks 13
2. Greek and Roman Versification compared 14
I. GREEK. — 3. Hexameter and Pentameter 15
    4. Archilochus 17
    5. Æolic Lyric Poetry. — Anacreon, Hipponax, Ananius 17
    6. Doric Lyric Poetry 18
    7. The Attic Drama 20
    8. The Alexandrian and the Later Greek Poets. — Nonnus 23
II. ROMAN. — 9. The Earliest Period until Ennius 24
    10. Ennius, Lucilius, Accius 26
    11. Contemporaries of Cicero 28
    12. Augustan Age 29
    13. The First Centuries after Christ 32
    14. Antiquarian Tendency in Versification 33
III. — 15. Final State of Greek and Roman Versification 34
    16. Rhythmical Poetry 36

FIRST SECTION.

GENERAL INTRODUCTION.

1. Rhythm and Metre 37
2. Long and Short Syllables. Arsis and Thesis 38
3. Verse-feet. Basis. Anacrusis 38
4. Verse 40
5. Cæsura 42

	PAGE
6. Final Syllables	42
7. System. Strophe. Epode	43
8. Punctuation in Verse	43
9. Rhyme. Alliteration	46

SECOND SECTION.
On Peculiarities of the Foot.

10. Synapheia	48
11. Resolution of Thesis and Arsis	48

THIRD SECTION.
Description of the Most Important Metres, Strophes, and Systems.

12. Dactylic Metres	50
13. Anapæstic Metres	55
14. Iambic Metres	57
Iambics of Phædrus	60
15. Trochaic Metres	62
16. Ionici a Minori	64
17. Logaœdic Metres	64
18. Asynartete Verse (Mixed Measures)	66
19. The Elegiac Distich (Callinus, Archilochus)	67
20. The Lyric Strophes of Horace	67
21. Epodic Systems	71

FOURTH SECTION.
On Metrical Licenses.

22. Preface	74
23. Metrical Licenses	74

FIFTH SECTION.
On the Rhythmical Structure of the Verse.

24. General Remarks	77
25. Rhythmical Structure of the Hexameter and Pentameter	79
26. Rhythmical Structure of the Remaining Metres	83

SIXTH SECTION.
Enclisis and Tmesis.

27. Enclisis	86
28. Tmesis	87

SEVENTH SECTION.

ON THE TREATMENT OF SUCCESSIVE VOWEL SOUNDS.

	PAGE
29. Synizesis, Diæresis, Crasis, Elision, Hiatus.	89
30. Synizesis in Greek	92
31. Synizesis in Latin	93
32. Diæresis	95
33. Elision	96
34. Elision in Greek. Crasis. Aphæresis	97
35. Elision in Latin	98
36. Differences in Elision in Greek and Latin Verse	101
37. Hiatus	103
38. Hiatus in Greek	104
39. Hiatus in Latin	106

EIGHTH SECTION.

LENGTHENING BY POSITION.

40. General Remarks	108
41. Greek	108
42. Latin	109

NINTH SECTION.

HOMERIC PROSODY.

43. Peculiarities of Prosody in Homer	111

TENTH SECTION.

LATIN PROSODY.

44. Peculiarities of Latin Prosody	112

ELEVENTH SECTION.

LENGTHENING.

45. Lengthening by the Thesis at the End of a Word	116
46. Greek	116
47. Latin	117
ALPHABETICAL INDEX	119

INTRODUCTION.

DEVELOPMENT OF CLASSICAL VERSIFICATION.

1. General Remarks.

In both Greek and Latin poetry versification depends solely upon the length of the single syllable; that is, upon the principle of quantity. The versification of the classic peoples developed in precisely the same way as the plastic art of the Greeks, and for the metrical form of language, originality did not appear to the poets to be the most important requirement. Rather was it the rule that when an exceptional genius had discovered the metrical form best adapted to a particular kind of poetry, this should be preserved; and poets preferred developing in details the approved invention of another, to supplanting it by a new and perhaps less suitable form.

Thus the Dactylic Hexameter became, through Homer, the accepted epic verse of all antiquity, and the Iambic Trimeter and the Trochaic Tetrameter Catalectic, both of which had their origin at the country festivals of the Ionians, remained the favorite metres of the dialogue of tragedy and comedy, products also of those same festivals, long after these had developed into artistic poetical form. The younger generation of Athenian tragedians followed the metrical example of the great masters — Æschylus, Sophocles, and Euripides.

For this reason a continuous, though not always equally

active and intelligent, tradition of metrical art runs throughout antiquity. This was greatly furthered by the guilds of poets formed in the centres of ancient culture, *e.g.* Athens, Alexandria, and Rome; and again after the time of Alexander the Great, by the care of the grammarians, who not only carefully analyzed the versification of the classical poets, but also kept up uninterrupted intercourse with poets.

2. Greek and Roman Versification compared.

If the Greek versification of the classical age, down to the time of Alexander the Great, is compared with the Latin up to Hadrian's time, it will be seen that the Greek versification is distinguished by originality, boldness, versatility, grace, and variability, in consequence of which characteristics it sometimes falls into arbitrary and irregular forms (though the Greek poets, and even Homer himself, are much stricter in their versification than was formerly supposed), while the Latin is distinguished by earnestness, dignity, and strictness of rule, which descends to the minutest detail, as well as by a clear understanding and judicious application of this strictness. This was well suited to the peculiarities of the Latin language, the strong, energetic, and sonorous, but much less rich and variable, sister tongue of the Greek; although, as a result, Latin verse sometimes suffered from monotony, pedantry, and excessive care.

In the choice of metres for the different kinds of poetry the Greeks usually surpassed the Romans in taste, as it is generally the case that in the artificial imitation of the metres of another people mistakes in use easily arise. During the classical period of Roman poetry it is especially the polymetrical forms of verse of the contemporaries of Cicero that show uncertainty and misconception in this respect.

I. GREEK.

3. Hexameter and Pentameter.

The oldest verse measure of a people is naturally κατὰ στίχον; that is, it consists of one verse, recurring as often as the poet pleases.

The first measure artistically developed among the Greeks was the Dactylic Hexameter. Its inventor, who belonged to the Ionic stock, is unknown.[1]

The lightness and mobility of the Ionic dialect; its richness in short syllables; the possibility of increasing still more the number of these short syllables, by placing long final vowels in a hiatus; the possibility, on the other hand, of lengthening short vowels by position, or at the close of words by the thesis; the varying quantity of many syllables, and the substitution of a long syllable for a pyrrhic arsis, — produced the rapid and peculiar development of this metre, of which the oldest representatives are the Homeric Hymns (about 900 B.C.) and the poems of Hesiod, and of the Homeric and Hesiodic school (about 800 B.C.).

Monotony of rhythm in the Hexameter is avoided by the change from dactyl to spondee, and by the different cæsuras.

This metre continued to hold its place in general popularity, and, until the end of the Middle Ages, was used in the most different kinds of poetry. Sanctioned by the authority of the Homeric poems, it influenced not only the dactylic measures, but also the other different metres. Still the authority of

---

[1] The ancients frequently confuse the inventor of a measure with the poet who first introduced it in literature, and so metres are often named, not after their inventors, but after the poet by whom they were most frequently employed.

Homer stood very much in the way of the proper development of the Hexameter from a popular to an artistic form, because in later times Homer's metrical rules and licenses were partially imitated, while the linguistic phenomena which occasioned them were in large part not understood; *e.g.* there was no knowledge of the *digamma æolicum* as used by Homer. The evil became still worse in this respect, that the Alexandrian poets evolved from misunderstood passages in Homer a mass of absurd rules or exceptions, as *e.g.* the hypermetric Hexameter, and a new metre, the *Hexameter myurus:* —

$$-\cup\cup\ -\cup\cup\ -\cup\cup\ -\cup\cup\ -\cup\cup\ \cup\cup$$

Their theories in turn served as models for the Greek and Roman poets.

The Pentameter was produced by repeating the first half of the Hexameter as far as the penthemimeral cæsura. Hexameter and Pentameter together formed the first verse system, the Distich, which appears for the first time in the work of the Ionic poets Callinus and Archilochus (about 700 B.C.). Through this change of metre the verse itself became more lively and passionate than in the unvarying Hexameter, and consequently the Distich resulted in giving more room for the subjectivity of the poet, and paved the way for lyric poetry.

The Distich was the beginning of strophic forms, and it shows already the harmonious and artistic finish which every strophe of the Golden Age of Greek literature has, even if, in the strophes of the Doric lyric poets and the dramatists, the difficulty of their formation and the great corruption of the text often prevent us from completely appreciating the skill displayed in their composition.

4. Archilochus.

From early times it had been customary at harvest festivals and vintage time to recite or sing songs of a joking or mocking sort, usually written in alternate form, in which Iambic and Trochaic metres were employed. In these measures the thesis was not fixed, but could be resolved; and in certain positions of the arsis a short vowel could be replaced at pleasure by a long. These metres came forth from obscurity into use at about the same time as the Distich, through the poems of one of the greatest artists of antiquity, — Archilochus of Paros, — who with perfect artistic knowledge used the Iambic Trimeter and Trochaic Tetrameter Catalectic in their greatest beauty. He also employed various iambic and dactylic metres, dactyls with anacrusis, asynartetic verses, made up by a combination of dactylic and iambic or trochaic measures. At the same time he developed the Epodic System, particularly by a union of iambic trimeters and dimeters, but also from dactylic or asynartetic and iambic (probably also trochaic) verses, and *vice versa*.

5. Æolic Lyric Poetry. — Anacreon. Hipponax. Ananius.

After Archilochus Greek versification made very rapid progress. Among those especially influential in its development were the Æolic poets Alcæus and Sappho (about 600 B.C.), who were the first to compose real strophes, consisting usually of two or four verses, of which two at least were alike, so that the metrical elements of the corresponding verses of the strophes were in general quite alike, except for single licenses in the basis, anacrusis, or middle of the verse. These poets seldom employed purely dactylic verse either in strophic or non-strophic poems, but more frequently such verse preceded by a dissyllabic beat of any quantity, even pyrrhic,—seldom iambic or trochaic,—apparently without a resolution of the thesis, but especially logaœdic, *ionici a minori* (sometimes also *a majori*, in combination with trochees), asynartetic measures, and mixed metres in great variety. The most remarkable of their strophes are the Sapphic, Alcaic, and Asclepiadean. The Æolic poets exercised great influence, especially on the Alexandrians and the Romans; *e.g.* the metre invented by Sappho, but named *hendecasyllabus phalæcius*, after an Alexandrian poet, was very often employed by both.

Anacreon, an Ionian of Teos (about 550 B.C.), stands about midway between the versification of Archilochus and that of Alcæus and Sappho. The effeminacy of his nature appears especially in his frequent use of *ionici a minori*, Glyconics, and the Anacreontic measures, named after himself. On the other hand, in other fragments, he appears as *numeros animosque secutus Archilochi*. In the formation of systems or strophes he was very fond of using Glyconic and Pherecratean measures. The spurious collection of poems which goes under his name is of no consequence in the discussion of his metrical forms. At about this same time the Ionians Hipponax and Ananius gave to the Iambic Trimeter and Trochaic Tetrameter Catalectic a new form by changing, in a curious way, the last iambus into a spondee, accented on the second syllable like the original iambus.

These "limping iambics" found great favor among the Alexandrians and Romans.

6. Doric Lyric Poetry.

The freest and boldest development of Greek lyric poetry took place among the Dorians. While the Æolic and Ionic lyrics were intended primarily to be rendered by soloists, the Dorians wrote their songs principally to be sung by the chorus on sacred or holiday occasions, so that one of these poets, Stesichorus, is said to have derived his name from this custom.

The Doric (like the dramatic) lyrical poetry preferred in general strophes of five or more verses, seldom over twenty, skilfully combined out of metres differing both in compass and component parts. In this way it happened that two or three shorter verses, or parts of verses, were united into one verse (Periods).

The antistrophe corresponds exactly to the strophe. After the time of Stesichorus the antistrophe was often followed by the epode, to which the following epodes must exactly correspond.

In contrast with the vivacity of the Ionians and the passion of the Æolians, the lyric poetry of the Dorians is characterized by earnestness, dignity, and calm in a degree appropriate to its object.

Alcman is considered the father of Doric lyric poetry (about 612 B.C.). He was followed by Stesichorus, Arion, Ibycus, Simonides, Bacchylides, and finally Pindar about 480 B.C., the only Doric lyric poet from whom complete poems have come down to us.

The last offshoot of Greek lyric poetry is the Dithyramb, originating in the worship of Bacchus, and characterized by the boldness and variety of its metres. It was introduced into literature by Arion (about 600 B.C.).

Although this metre also was at first antistrophic, after the year 400 B.C. the antistrophe fell away, and in consequence of this the Dithyramb degenerated into such looseness that by the irregularity of its structure it seems to have passed from the highest point of thought and metre into mere prose.

7. The Attic Drama.

The drama that has developed out of the songs and dances of country festivals is a combination of epic and lyric poetry of such a kind that the dialogue parts representing the action of the play form the epic element; and the songs of the chorus or of individual members of the chorus or of the actors, the lyrical.

In a corresponding way, as regards the metres, the dialogue is usually written in iambic or trochaic verses (especially iambic trimeter, more rarely trochaic tetrameter catalectic, in comedy frequently in iambic tetrameter catalectic); and the songs in lyric metres, partly those used by the earlier lyric poets, and partly new and free inventions of the dramatists appropriate to the situation.

Excellent evidence to show how the dramatists regarded the harmony and adaptation of the metre is found in their *Stichomythy*; that is, the frequent cases where question and answer correspond with each other exactly in compass (usually one verse, sometimes two or more).

The songs of the whole chorus which enters when the action has reached a point of rest or change, and also marks the end of an act, are characterized by the calmness and dignity of the rhythm. The songs of the individual members of the chorus and the actors show more liveliness, excitement, and variation, especially in Euripides, and frequently lack the antistrophic form (ἀπολελυμένα).

The metrical style of Æschylus is strict and regular, sometimes even harsh and rigid. The versification of Euripides is free and graceful, though often careless and arbitrary, or showing a striving after effect. These faults are particularly conspicuous in the lyrical parts, however much they may please us by the change of measures and variety of rhythm.

Sophocles stands, in respect to metre, midway between the two; but, in general with the year 424 B.C., the metre of the tragedians becomes freer and less exact, as is shown by the Philoctetes of Sophocles and the later dramas of Euripides.

Euripides, who differs strikingly in the metres of the dialogue, and still more in the lyrical parts, from his predecessors, has had the greatest influence upon the later writers of Attic tragedy.

Among the comedians, Aristophanes far surpassed all others in wealth of expression, skill, and tasteful employment of metrical forms, and was for this reason ranked by antiquity with Archilochus. It goes without saying that the versification of tragedy is distinguished from that of comedy by its greater force and dignity, while the rhythm of comedy is gayer and freer. This fact is apparent not only in the choruses but also in the dialogue, and particularly noticeable in the ready admission of anapæsts in all the feet of the comic trimeter except the last.

The epode rarely occurs in tragedy, and not always, as in the lyrical poetry of the Dorians, after one pair of strophes, but even after two or three, though without epodic correspondence taking place, as in Pindar.

The dramatists were very fond of the anapæstic metre, which had been used in marching-songs by the Spartans from earliest times. It was often employed, partly in choruses, especially where there was some movement of the chorus or announcement by the leader of the chorus, and partly in the songs of the actors, particularly where these expressed sorrow or complaint.

The anapæstic system consists of dimeters interspersed with monometers, and forms usually the close of the catalectic dimeter (*versus paroemiacus*).—The catalectic tetrameter was used only in comedy.

The lyrical portions, especially the strophes and antistrophes, show the same variety of metres as the Doric lyric poetry.

Along with iambic and trochaic rhythms, which are used with peculiar licenses in the resolution of the thesis, neglect of the cæsura, suppression of the arsis, etc., which are not allowed in the dialogues, we find also dactylic measures, often with anacrusis, epitrites, cretics, pæons, *ionici a minori* (not *a majori*), dactylo-trochees, seldom dactylo-epitrites, bacchics, and other verses.

The dochmiac rhythm deserves special mention, of which the original forms, as well as the most usual, are these: —

$$\cup \overset{\_}{\overset{\cup}{\_}} \overset{\_}{\_} \cup \overset{\_}{\_}$$
$$\overset{\_}{\_} \cup \cup \overset{\_}{\_} \cup \overset{\_}{\_}$$

From this were developed numerous other forms by resolution of the theses and by replacing the short syllable preceding the last by a long.

The dochmiac measure is sometimes combined with the cretic and trochaic, seldom with the bacchic and logaœdic, and most frequently with the iambic. It occurs rarely in the comedians, and still more rarely among the Dorians, but very frequently in tragedy, especially to express complaint and pain.

Among the logaœdic verses, the favorite metres were the Glyconic and Pherecratean, partly in the stricter form of Anacreon, partly in the manner of the Dorians (with great freedom in the structure of the basis), and partly, after

Sophocles, with transposition of the dactyl in polyschematic form. Not infrequently, as among the Dorians, shorter verses, or parts of verses, were united to form a longer verse or period. In the fourth century the choral lyrical part of tragedy degenerated, in the same way as the dithyramb, into looseness and trifling (illustrated by Chæremon); the Middle and New Comedy lacked the chorus, although not the lyric measures.

8. The Alexandrian and the Later Greek Poets.— Nonnus.

The independent development of Greek versification extends to about the age of Alexander the Great (330 B.C.). In the following, so-called Alexandrian (330–30 B.C.), as well as in the Roman and Byzantine periods, hardly any addition was made to the previous stock of metres. The Sotadeus, indeed,

$$\acute{-}\acute{-}\cup\cup\ \acute{-}\acute{-}\cup\cup\ \acute{-}\acute{-}\cup\cup\ \acute{-}\acute{-}$$

was an invention of the Alexandrians; but in point of fact the old Greeks had created such an astonishing number of different sorts of metres, systems, and strophes, that any increase was scarcely possible. The later Greeks restricted this metrical wealth, since in general they limited themselves to a comparatively small number of metres and short systems or strophes, and usually imitated in a mechanical way the Ionic and Æolic poets. Poetry written κατὰ στίχον predominated, just as it did among the Romans after Augustus, and in this manner the Greeks as well as the Romans often employed verses which previously had formed parts of a system.

A marked peculiarity of the Alexandrian and later poets was the tendency towards artificial verses, the most remarkable examples of which are found in the poems of Simmias, Dosiadas, and Besantinus (Anthologia Lyrica, ed. Bergk p. 511 sqq.). Another peculiarity was a great, and often pedantic and affected, carefulness in the structure of their favorite metres, in which attempt they were powerfully assisted by the grammarians, and, in fact, often led astray by their false theories.

Almost at the end of Greek literature in the fifth century A.D., probably under the influence of Roman versification, Nonnus wrote hexameter verse of remarkable strictness and consistency, though not always with success, inasmuch as he had a decided preference for the dactyl (always in the fifth foot), made the τομὴ κατὰ τρίτον τροχαῖον the ruling pause, avoided a word-end in the fourth trochee, introduced once more the strict rules of position, greatly limited cases of elision, and still more cases of hiatus, and gave up lengthening short final syllables in the thesis. Though the next succeeding poets followed his example, Nonnus lived too late to effect any thorough reform in Greek versification. While music and dancing or rhythmical movements of the body were inseparable from the lyrical poetry of the old Greeks, after the Alexandrian period versification and music were sharply distinguished. The later Greek poets, even the dramatists, intended their works principally for reading or recitation without musical accompaniment.

II. ROMAN.

9. The Earliest Period until Ennius.

The oldest metre of the Romans was the Saturnian,

The Earliest Period until Ennius.   25

whose original form was made up by combining an iambic and trochaic series: —

$$\cup \perp \cup \perp \cup \perp \cup \mid \perp \cup \perp \cup \perp \cup$$

malum dabunt Metelli Naevio poetae.

This verse, which in course of time became confused on account of neglect of the caesura and frequent suppression of the third, and especially the sixth, arsis, could not, after the Punic wars, satisfy the artistic feeling of the Romans. It vanished with Naevius (died about 200 B.C.), although it was occasionally employed by later poets, like Accius, Varro, and Terentianus Maurus, in learned imitation of their predecessors.

Since on occasions of public and private festivity, the *ludi scaenici* were presented as well as the *ludi circenses*, Livius Andronicus (after 240 B.C.), and his successors in tragedy and comedy, — Naevius, Plautus, Terence, Ennius, Pacuvius, Accius, and others, — appropriated the scenic metres of the Greek drama, iambic, trochaic, anapaestic, cretic, bacchic, occasionally also dactylic, yet with the greatest licenses; as *e.g.* the short arsis in iambics and trochees could always be lengthened, except in the last iambic foot. In the resolution of the thesis and arsis, in the use of elision and synizesis, and in other respects, they often transgressed the rules. Further, in prosody they made use of many irregularities, occasioned by the archaic or plebeian pronunciation of the Latin language which had been so long neglected.

In the dialogue parts the Romans, like the Greeks, used principally the iambic trimeter and trochaic tetrameter catalectic, and in comedy the iambic tetrameter catalectic also. These metres attained a comparatively high degree of finish, while the other iambic and trochaic metres, still more the cretic and bacchic, and the anapæstic most of all, remained in a very rude stage of development.

There was no chorus in Latin drama until the time of Augustus, but there were lyrical passages (*cantica*) sung by the actors, which were usually written in anapæstic, cretic, and bacchic metres. In general the old dramatists, up to the end of the Republic, and particularly after the year 150 B.C., influenced by the contemporaneous dactylic poets, show a continual effort after a greater development of their art. On the other hand, the number of their metres steadily decreased, as is shown by a comparison of Plautus and Terence, so that finally the principal metres employed in the drama were the iambic trimeter and the trochaic tetrameter catalectic, which were universally popular.

The last representative of the old iambic versification was the fabulist Phædrus (about 50 A.D.), who, in view of the Proverbs of Syrus, then much in vogue, admitted in his own fables, which were also devoted to ethical purposes, the spondee in the even feet of the iambic trimeter, but elsewhere showed almost nothing of the peculiarities of Plautus and Terence. Iambic and trochaic poetry, with the same free use of the spondee, appears occasionally in the antiquarian period of the Frontonians (about 150 A.D.) and at the end of Roman literature, in consequence of the increasing decadence of culture.

10. Ennius. Lucilius. Accius.

As there was some reason to fear that the Latin language would again degenerate into the rudeness of the Saturnian verse through the irregularity of the dramatic metres and prosody, great credit is due to Ennius (239-169 B.C.) for his introduction of the dactylic hexameter, imitated with care and general good taste from Homer. Resolution of the thesis was excluded from Ennius' hexameter, and he adhered as closely as possible to the model of the Greeks in matters of prosody, as the prosody of Latin had been originally homogeneous with that of Greek, and had degenerated only after the lapse of time. Ennius still retained the original long quantity of the final syllables in *at*, *et*, *it* (2d pers. *ās*, *ēs*, *is*), as well as the contemporaneous dramatists. Further, Ennius employed in his Satires the elegiac distich, besides the most common metres of the dramatists, the iambic trimeter and the trochaic tetrameter catalectic, and finally, in imitation of the Alexandrians, the wonderful Sotadic measure, though with various licenses.

Although there are cases of harshness, the great majority of Ennius' hexameters are of remarkable beauty, because of the evident genius of the poet, who *e.g.* has far fewer cases of elision in the *Annales* than any poet of the Republic, and also because of his rich and comprehensive knowledge of Latin, Greek, and Oscan; but above all, because of the fact that Roman versification already before Ennius had followed the quantitative principle exclusively, so that he had only to remove the abuses of prosody which had crept in during the rude state of the language between 350 and 250 B.C. It is quite evident that Ennius attempted to direct the attention of Roman poets to the strictness and consistency of the metrical art. He exercised an immense influence over all later writers, the more so because, until Vergil's time, his much-praised epic, the *Annales*, was the most popular glorification of the heroic deeds of the old Romans.

Next followed the satirist Lucilius, who employed the hexameter principally, besides the other metres used by Ennius, in his Satires, though he disdained the Sotadic. He marks an advance in metrical art, although there is no lack of harsh usages which are partially excused by the light colloquial tone of satire. Accius, in his non-dramatic poetry, followed the metrical principles of Ennius.

11. Contemporaries of Cicero.

Until the time of Cicero the dactylic poets contented themselves with the metres employed by Ennius; but they zealously furthered their artistic development. The most perfect example of this effort is the poem of Lucretius, composed correctly and according to rule, but without grace and variety of rhythm.

The younger contemporaries of Cicero, led by Lævius, like Catullus, Calvus, and others, disdained that simplicity, and introduced into Roman poetry a great number of metres, mostly or wholly borrowed from the Alexandrians, and which they used in general with great skill. Of course the hexameter was not neglected (cf. Varro Atacinus), but the distich remained undeveloped. Catullus was the first among the Romans to show attention to the Æolic poetry, by imitating Sappho. It is possible also that he was somewhat influenced by Anacreon. The Horatian epode was not unknown to this period; on the contrary, in imitation of the Alexandrians, poets already formed iambic and trochaic metres of various kinds according to the strict metrical laws of the Greeks; indeed, pure iambic lines with complete exclusion of every other foot.

Hipponactean Iambics and Hendecasyllabic Phalæceans were particular favorites.

Between Lucretius and Catullus, beside Laevius, stood Varro Reatinus, who shows in his Satires, in imitation of the Alexandrians, great skill together with great variety of versification. He also employed iambic, trochaic, and Sotadic verses with the freedom of Ennius and Lucilius.

The verse-systems found in Catullus are the two-lined Asclepiadean, the four-lined Sapphic, and two Glyconics closing with a Pherecratean, one four-lined, and one consisting of three and two lines.

Catullus' versification had imitators and friends even in the Augustan Age, and in the first century A.D. His great variety of metres did not meet with general approval. The Phalaecean continued to be popular until the end of Roman literature, and the Hipponactean until the time of Trajan, though both were more strictly treated.

12. Augustan Age.

The age of Augustus (40 B.C. to 14 A.D.) brought the development of Roman metre to a close.

The hexameter was brought to its highest perfection by Vergil and Ovid. Vergil, indeed, believed that he could not wholly eliminate the licenses which the older Romans, especially Ennius, had allowed in respect to the rhythmical laws of the hexameter, harsh elision and hiatus, synizesis, lengthening of a final syllable in the thesis, etc. But he used them rarely and moderately, usually only to paint the situation by the rhythm of the verse, — an art in which he is a master. Unfortunately, his versification is sometimes disfigured by a pedantic imitation of the Alexandrian philologists where they had misunderstood Homeric verses.

Ovid diminished still more the number of licenses which Vergil had allowed, so that, although the hexameters of the

Metamorphoses are somewhat freer than the elegiacs, his verses, considered singly, are the most beautiful models of harmony and metrical skill.

If read for any length of time, however, they grow tiresome because of their too great similarity, especially as Ovid comparatively seldom makes use of that rhythmical portraiture in which Vergil was so skilful.

In the hexameter of Satire, which was distinguished from the prose language of the educated only by its metre, Horace preserved the licenses of Lucilius, but lessened his harshness. The verse of the Epistles, especially of the second book, is considerably more polished than that of the Satires. As would be expected in this sort of poetry, the licenses borrowed from the Greeks by poets of the higher style, *e.g.* hiatus and a spondee in the fifth foot, are almost wholly avoided.

The distich also, which in Catullus still appeared rude, was perfected by Tibullus, by Propertius in his later works, and particularly by Ovid, although the latter, in the works written during his exile, dropped something of the metrical strictness shown in his erotic poetry.

Horace introduced the epodic versification of Archilochus into Roman poetry, and also the lyrical measures of the Æolic poets Alcæus and Sappho. Archilochus and Anacreon also may have had some influence on the versification of the Odes. It is not certain whether the two metres not met with in Greek (Od. I. 8; Ep. 13), were invented by Horace or not; also whether the division of the strophes into four lines, which is the universal rule in the Odes,—for Od. IV. 8 is interpolated,—was borrowed from Alcæus or not.

In general, we are in the dark about the origin of many

of the strophes of Horace, on account of the loss of his Greek models and the contradictory statements of the Latin grammarians.

On the other hand, Horace paid full regard to the spirit of the Latin language, partly by setting aside, and partly by reducing to a very small number, those licenses which the Æolic poets had allowed themselves in respect to cæsura and *syllaba anceps*, and consequently his metres became more equal and dignified. Thus, for instance, the Asclepiads and the eleven-syllabled Alcaics and Sapphics received a firmly fixed cæsura. In the Asclepiads the basis was always a spondee, and the Alcaic and Sapphic verses had a spondee always before the cæsura. Still Horace has more cases of elision in his lyrical measures than the tragedian Seneca, and further allows monosyllabic conjunctions and prepositions at the cæsura and at the end of the verse, contrary to Seneca's usage. No advance was ever made by the Romans beyond the lyrical versification of Horace. The attempt, condemned by Horace, but made by his contemporaries, to imitate the Odes of Pindar, found no sympathy.

In the time of Augustus, tragedy, which had been zealously cultivated in opposition to comedy, was emancipated from the metrical traditions of the Republic, and its iambics and trochaics were constructed according to the model of the Greek tragedians, and the rule adopted from the Alexandrians, that the foot preceding the last iambus in the iambic trimeter and trochaic tetrameter catalectic must necessarily be a spondee or an anapæst. In general, much greater freedom was allowed the anapæst in iambic trimeter in Latin tragedy than in Greek. At the same time the chorus was introduced,—that is, in the manner of Euripides,—

with a loose relation to the action of the drama from which was taken only a point of departure for general descriptions and reflections. In these choruses anapæstic monometers were employed in a most unartistic manner, besides the dactylic and logaœdic metres illustrated in Seneca.

13. The First Centuries after Christ.

The first century after Christ, until Hadrian (117), represents the Alexandrian period of Roman versification. No further enrichment was made, and there were but few attempts to employ a great number of metres. Poets contented themselves with a consistent and tasteful though not infrequently pedantic improvement of the metres already in use.

The grammarians were responsible for many false explanations of the metrical peculiarities of Vergil, who was studied with equal zeal, and enjoyed the same authority among the Romans as Homer among the Greeks, although their erroneous theories exercised little influence over the better poets even to the end of the fourth century, as is shown by Claudianus and Rutilius Namatianus in the time of Honorius. Moreover, it was unfortunate that the taste for the four-lined strophes of Horace, with the exception of the ever-popular Sapphic, disappeared so quickly, as the choruses of Seneca prove. Instead, poets began to use the lyrical measures of Horace in poetry written κατὰ στίχον. In a very peculiar manner Seneca, in two tragedies (Agamemnon and Œdipus), combined freer chorus songs out of the short verses or portions of verses of Horace. In the last centuries this custom of making new verses out of parts of Horatian metres became more common. In other respects the metrical art was very carefully developed in the most minute details, so that licenses which were common in the Augustan poets became rare, and those which were infrequent in the Augustan poetry were almost unknown.

The post-Augustan poets generally took Vergil and Ovid for their models, but gave the most weight to Ovid's example. For as his distich was the pattern for most of them, so his influence was very considerable on the form of the other dactylic and logaoedic metres. In other lines Horace's lyrical and satirical metres were models. Remark has already been made about Catullus' influence (cf. **11**).

Here, too, must be mentioned that tendency, noticed already among the later Greeks, towards playing with words and affectations, which became stronger and stronger, the more the want of real substance in poetry was felt. The most remarkable example, unique in its kind, of this tendency is the poetry of Porfyrius Optatianus (about 330).

14. Antiquarian Tendency in Versification.

After the time of Hadrian and Fronto an antiquarian tendency made its influence felt in Roman poetry, together with the steady imitation of Augustan versification, so that occasionally not only iambic and trochaic verses were written with the metrical (not prosodical) licenses of Plautus, but also poets returned to the metrical variety of Lævius and Catullus, as is seen in Septimius Serenus and Terentianus Maurus, poets of the third century. Their example was followed by the Christian writers after the fourth century, although they also employed the verses of Horace in their poetry.

III.

15. Final State of Greek and Roman Versification.

The state of both Greek and Roman versification after the third century is so nearly the same that the subject can be treated as one.

In both languages the most common metres continued to be the dactylic hexameter and pentameter, as well as various iambic and trochaic verses; in Greek the iambic trimeter, in Latin the trochaic tetrameter catalectic and the iambic dimeter, partly κατὰ στίχον, partly in strophes.

As is shown by the latest ancient and by the mediæval Greek and Roman poets, all appreciation of the strophe which, in ancient times, had represented the harmonious combination of different verses into one artistic whole, had vanished. All combinations of like or unlike verses, repeated in the same succession of verses and in the same numbers, if only they had a decided stop at the end, were considered as strophes. Such "strophes" were especially used for religious purposes (Christian hymns). In the structure of these hymns, among the Greeks after Gregorius Nazianzenus (360), the most serviceable metre was the iambic trimeter, and sometimes the catalectic iambic dimeter and Anacreontics: among the Romans the most used metres were the iambic dimeter and the catalectic trochaic tetrameter.

At this same time men began to lose the exact appreciation of the peculiar appropriateness of each metre. From the third century Roman poets (Alfius Avitus, and later Festus Avienus) had employed iambic metres in epic representation, and the same thing was done in Greek in the seventh century by Georgius Pisides. On the other hand, after the same date, Latin tragedies (Medea and Orestes) had been written in hexameter. So, too, in lyric poetry little taste was shown in the choice of metres, as we see in the case of Ausonius and Prudentius about 400 A.D.

When after the third century thorough culture and, together with that, the appreciation of language declined, the erroneous theories of the grammarians exercised continually greater influence on the ancient versification, and, further, many Roman poets, especially the Christians, began to neglect quantities, at first in proper names, particularly Greek, or in long words which were unsuited to the verse. This became much worse in the Middle Ages, though here, too, the poets were very different according to their time and training. Among the Greeks the laws of prosody were more strictly enforced. But the Byzantine poets, even the best of them after Georgius Pisides, allowed themselves to make the letters α, ι, υ, which have not different forms for long and short, either long or short, except when lengthened by a strong position; η and ω and the diphthongs were always long, ε and ο short, when a single consonant followed, and frequently when in weak position. Proper names and technical terms were treated very freely. The extinction of the old spirit of the language was shown in this fact that many Christian poets of Rome allowed no resolution of the thesis in iambic and trochaic feet, and in general avoided trisyllabic feet, as was the rule among the Greeks after Georgius Pisides.

Nevertheless, the quantitative poetry of the Middle Ages was strictly separated in the consciousness of the poets from the rhythmical. A remarkable proof of this lies in the fact that the Byzantine poets who observed the principle of quantity, when writing in iambics, always had a paroxytone word at the end of the trimeter. They wished thus to show that their verse took no account of grammatical accent, but rather that in the manner of the ancients the rhythmical accent differed as much as possible from the grammatical.

16. Rhythmical Poetry.

On account of the extinction of the appreciation of long and short syllables, there was developed among the Romans after the third century, and among the Greeks in the first half of the Middle Ages when not earlier, the so-called rhythmical poetry, which, being steadily emancipated from the rules of prosody, though at first observing rhythmical laws, led naturally to the observance of the grammatical accent in certain cases, and restored, in Latin, beside the dactylic hexameter, generally popular iambic and trochaic metres, especially the iambic dimeter and catalectic trochaic tetrameter; in Greek it restored the *iambicus septenarius*, which had always been popular, the so-called *versus politicus*, which always consisted of fifteen syllables. This metre was very common among the educated also after the twelfth century. In this, as in the rhythmical verses of the Romans, the cæsura was generally retained (*e.g.* in the *versus politicus* after the fourth thesis), just as was usual in metrical poetry. The same remarks apply to the strophes of rhythmical poetry that were made above, about the metrical strophes of the end of antiquity and of the Middle Ages.

The last thing to be noticed is, that in most of the Greek and Latin poets of the Middle Ages all appreciation of the difference between poetic and prosaic productions was lost. Everything possible was written in verse, even such themes as lie farthest distant from real poetry.

FIRST SECTION.

GENERAL INTRODUCTION.

1. Rhythm and Metre.

THE euphony of the classical languages depends, in prose, upon the Rhythm (*numerus*); that is, upon a grouping of the words of the sentence, especially at its beginning and end, which is harmonious and pleasing to the ear. In poetry it depends upon the Metre; that is, the artistic combination of long and short syllables in verse, system, or strophe.

In olden times, in the structure of verse, the *principle of quantity* was the only one considered; that is, the words making up the verse were measured according to the length of their vowels. The prose accent, as well as the logical importance of the words, or parts of words, was not taken into consideration.

The combination of a raising and a lowering of the voice forms the verse-foot.

The poets, too, followed the rules of rhythm partly by causing the accentuation of the verse-feet to vary as much as possible from the prose pronunciation of the words, partly by harmoniously joining the parts of the verse so that the compass of the individual words might differ as much as possible from that of the single verse-feet, and partly by using at the end of each metrical series — as well of the divisions of the verse caused by the cæsura as at the end of every artificial combination of verse-feet — the kind of verse-foot peculiar to this end.

2. Long and Short Syllables. Arsis and Thesis.

Every vowel of a Greek or Latin word has an exact time (χρόνος, *tempus*), and is either long or short, — with the exception of those cases, rare in prose, but more common in poetry, where the same vowel can be at the same time either long or short.

A vowel is either long by nature or it is regarded as long on account of its position before two or more consonants. In *versification*, one long is equivalent to two short syllables.

A *complete verse-foot* has at least one raising (*Thesis*) and one lowering (*Arsis*) of tone, produced by a greater or less stress of the voice. The Thesis is always long, except when it is resolved into two short syllables. The Arsis is sometimes short, sometimes long.

To *scan* is to read the verse according to the Thesis and Arsis.

3. Verse-feet. Basis. Anacrusis.

The most common combinations of syllables, or verse-feet, are the following: —

∪ ∪	Pyrrhic	lĕgĭt	♪ ♪
_ ∪	Trochee	lēgĭt	♩ ♪
∪ _	Iambus	dŭcēs	♪ ♩
_ _	Spondee	lēgī	♩ ♩

Verse-feet. 39

Meter		Name		Example	
⏑ ⏑ ⏑	....	Tribrach	....	*lĕgĭtĕ*	....
— ⏑ ⏑	....	Dactyl	....	*lĕgĭmŭs*	....
⏑ ⏑ —	....	Anapæst	....	*lĕgĕrēnt*	....
⏑ — ⏑	....	Amphibrachus { (*sŭpĕrnĕ* in Lucr.) / *ĕgōnĕ* }			...
⏑ — —	..	{ Bacchius / Antibacchius / Palimbacchius }	..	*ămīcōs*	....
— — ⏑	..	{ Antibacchius / Palimbacchius / Bacchius }	..	*lēgīstīs*	....
— ⏑ —	..	{ Cretic / Amphimacer }	..	*cōnsŭlēs*	....
— — —	....	Molossus	....	*lēgērūnt*	....
⏑ ⏑ ⏑ ⏑	....	Proceleusmaticus	..	*ănĭmŭlă*	....
— ⏑ ⏑ ⏑	....	Pæon *primus*	.....	*cōnsŭlĭbŭs*	......
⏑ — ⏑ ⏑	....	Pæon *secundus*	....	*lĕgēntĭbŭs*	.....
⏑ ⏑ — ⏑	....	Pæon *tertius*	......	*lĕgĭtōtĕ*	....
⏑ ⏑ ⏑ —	....	Pæon *quartus*	.....	*ĭtĭnĕrī*	....
⏑ ⏑ — —	....	Ionic *a minori*	....	*rĕtŭlīssēnt*	.....
— — ⏑ ⏑	....	Ionic *a majori*	....	*cōnfēcĕrāt*	......
— ⏑ ⏑ —	....	Choriambus	......	*cōntŭlĕrānt*	....
⏑ — — ⏑	....	Antispast	....	*lĕgēbārīs*	....
— ⏑ — ⏑	..	{ Ditrochee / Dichoreus }	......	*cōllĭgūntūr*	.....
⏑ — ⏑ —	....	Diiambus	....	*lĕgāmĭnī*	....
⏑ — — —	....	First Epitrite	.....	*rĕlēgērūnt*	......
— ⏑ — —	....	Second Epitrite	....	*ēlĭgēbānt*	......
— — ⏑ —	....	Third Epitrite	....	*sēlēgĕrīnt*	......
— — — ⏑	....	Fourth Epitrite	....	*cōllēgīstīs*	......
— — — —	....	Dispondee	....	*sēlĭgĕrūnt*	......
⏑ — — ⏑ —		Dochmius	....	*ămīcōs tĕnēs*	....

The combination of two feet is called a *Dipody*. Iambic, Trochaic, and Anapæstic verse, but not the Dactylic, is measured by Dipodies. The Iambic verse, containing six feet, is therefore called a *Trimeter*. The greatest stress of the metrical Ictus is laid upon the first part of the Dipody, consequently on the odd feet.

Basis is the term applied by later writers on metre to the dissyllabic prelude at the beginning of Phalæcean, Pherecratean, Asclepiadean, and other verses, which in Greek poetry consists of a Trochee, Spondee, Iambus, or Pyrrhic.

Anacrusis is the name given to the monosyllabic prelude before the first thesis of the Alcaic Hendecasyllabic and Enneasyllabic, and other verses. This syllable is either long or short.

4. Verse.

A *Verse* is a metrical series consisting of like or different feet, which, however, are not combined arbitrarily or mechanically, but according to the law of Symmetry and Euphony, as it presents itself to the artistic sense of the poet.

A Verse must not number over thirty *moræ* (a *mora* is the unit of measure, the time of one short syllable, a ♪ in music); although in lyric poetry and in the choruses of the Greek drama there are found longer combinations, so-called Periods, of which no account is taken in the following pages.

The metrical correctness of a verse — that is, the correct quantity of the syllables, the strict exclusion of all illegitimate feet — was a matter of course in the old poets until the degeneration of Latin and Greek literature; but metrical correctness by no means makes a verse a work of art, and it becomes such only by an exact keeping of the laws of rhythm, especially at the close of a metrical series. Moreover, a longer verse needs at least one definite division (Cæsura), which allows the voice to rest, and divides the verse symmetrically and harmoniously.

Again, it is a law of euphony that the same letter must not recur too frequently in the same verse, as in Ennius: —

> O Tite tute tibi tanta tyranne tulisti.

Just as much to be avoided are words of the same number of syllables, or those which are too long, as in Ennius and Namatianus: —

> sparsis hastis longis campus splendet et horret.
>
> Bellerophonteis sollicitudinibus.

On the contrary, there must be a proper mingling of longer and shorter words.

A verse of which the last foot is incomplete is called *Catalectic*. If this incomplete foot contains one syllable, it is called *Catalecticus in syllabam;* if two, *Catalecticus in disyllabum*.

A verse can be called *Hypercatalectic* if it has one or two arses after the last complete foot.

A verse is called *Simple* if it consists of like feet; *Compound*, if it consists of unlike feet.

A verse in which Dactyls and Trochees are used together is called *Logaœdic*.

Verses made up of two different metrical series are called *Asynartete*. At the end of the first series *hiatus* and *syllaba anceps* are generally allowed.

In view of the great artistic taste of the Greeks and Romans, and the highly finished state of their languages, it can be assumed that their most usual verse-feet were also the most perfect. As such, the Dactylic Hexameter and Pentameter, the Iambic Trimeter, the Trochaic Tetrameter Catalectic, the Anapæstic Dimeter and Tetrameter Catalectic, the Glyconic and Asclepiadean measures, and the Alcaic and Sapphic Strophes, are especially remarkable.

5. Cæsura.

In order to give the voice a rest, verses of more than ten syllables have usually one or two divisions (*Cæsura*, τομή); but this rest or pause is shorter than at the end of the verse.

Sometimes there is besides the Primary Cæsura a Secondary Cæsura, as *e.g.* in the Dactylic Hexameter we find the *Trithemimeres* (cæsura after the third half-foot), together with the *Hephthemimeres* (cæsura after the seventh half-foot).

The division of the parts of the verse by the cæsura is not accidental or mechanical, but depends upon the law of Symmetry and Euphony. Hence it often happens that the parts of the verse made by the cæsura (also called "Metrical Series") elsewhere appear as independent verses. This is also further explained by the fact that the cæsura usually occurs about in the middle of the verse.

The original metre is frequently cut in two by the cæsura. So *e.g.* the Penthemimeral and Hephthemimeral cæsuras in the Dactylic Hexameter fall upon an Anapæst; in the Iambic Trimeter, upon a Trochee. The greatest stress of the metrical ictus rests on the first half of the verse as far as the cæsura.

6. Final Syllables.

The *Final Syllable* of the verse is *common;* that is, it can be either long or short. Compare **10**.

For this syllable the law of Hiatus is not binding. Elision and the Apostrophe are not allowed at the end of the verse, except when several verses are united by Synapheia. In this case neither Syllaba Anceps nor Hiatus is admitted ; but Elision, and sometimes the division of a word at the end of the verse, occur. Compare 10.

For the so-called *Hexametri hypermetri*, compare 36.

7. System. Strophe. Epode.

A *System* is the combination of two or more verses so as to form an artistic rhythmical unity. Such Systems can be repeated as often as desired.

It is not necessary, and indeed quite seldom happens, that the parts of a System of verses should be united to each other by Synapheia.

If such a System is repeated one or more times, it is called a *Strophe*.

In Doric and dramatic lyrical poetry the even (second, fourth, etc.) Strophes are called *Antistrophes*.

Epode (*epodus*, ἐπῳδός, fem. gen.) is the name applied to the Verse-System which, in Doric lyric poetry and in the choruses of tragedy, follows the Antistrophe and closes this and the Strophe.

Epode (*epodus*, ἐπῳδός, masc. gen.) is also the name applied to a shorter or even a longer asynartete (Hor. Epod. 11, 13) verse, which is combined with the preceding into a System. Again, the combination of two such verses, with the exception of the Elegiac Distich, is called an Epode (Horace).

The repetition of Dactylic Distiches or Epodes is not considered as a Strophic structure.

8. Punctuation in Verse.

Since the Verse, the parts of the Verse produced by the cæsura, and the Verse-Systems, are merely a result of the euphony and rhythm of language, they have originally nothing to do with the logical structure of the sentence, as it is represented to the eye by punctuation. Hence it may happen in verses united by Synapheia, that *one* word belongs to two different verses. Therefore it is by no means necessary that the verse, the cæsura, or even the strophe or antistrophe and epode, should close at a point of punctuation, as *e.g.* Pindar and Horace show. Further, it introduces no difficulty that a word should stand at the end of a verse, or in the cæsura, which is to be closely connected with what follows. Thus we often find, *e.g.* in Horace at the end of lyric verses (except at the end of the strophe) and of the satiric Hexameter *et, aut, vel,* etc., or a monosyllabic preposition (as in the strophes of the Greeks).

Even a full stop before the last syllable is not avoided, as in Catullus:—

> quid? non est homo bellus? inquies? *est.*

and in Horace:—

> scitari libet ex ipso, quodcumque refers. *dic,*
> ad cenam veniat.

Still, the desire to make the metrical endings, marked out by the cæsura and close of the verse, coincide with the divisions of the sentence, as well as to avoid harsh discords, is so deeply implanted in our poetic instinct, that, at least in verses which are not united in system or strophe, the poets early (as Homer shows) directed their attention to this point. Therefore it seldom happens outside of the strophe, especially among the Greeks, that the last syllable or the last foot of a verse belongs to the following sentence. In the same way a full stop after the first syllable or the first foot of a verse is avoided.

Therefore such a case as Il. I. 51, 52:—

> αὐτὰρ ἔπειτ' αὐτοῖσι βέλος ἐχεπευκὲς ἐφιείς
> βάλλ'· αἰεὶ δὲ πυραὶ νεκύων καίοντο θαμεῖαι;

is not to be commended, although here the harshness is diminished by the logical importance of the first word and by the elision.

Vergil sometimes for the sake of effect ends a rather long speech with an initial dactyl. Æn. IV. 570:—

> femina.' sic fatus nocti se inmiscuit atrae.

The placing of a full stop at the distance of a half-foot before or after the principal caesura is also avoided, and hence such a verse as the following is faulty (Æn. I. 17):—

> hic currus *fuit;* hoc | regnum dea gentibus esse.

Still more this (Æn. VII. 635):—

> pulverulentus eques | *furit.* omnes arma requirunt.

So too these verses of Æschylus and Sophocles (Seven against Thebes, 1030; El. 1038):—

> ἀλλ' ὃν πόλις στυγεῖ, σὺ | τιμήσεις τάφῳ;
> ὅταν γὰρ εὖ φρονῇς, τόθ' ἡγήσει σὺ νῷν.

In Homer (Od. V. 234), on the other hand, we must write:—

> δῶκέν οἱ πέλεκυν, μέγαν, ἄρμενον ἐν παλάμῃσιν;

not:—
> πέλεκυν μέγαν.

Still, the tragedians, especially after Sophocles, allow themselves much freedom with respect to the disagreement of metre and punctuation, in order to increase the effect of passages in the dialogue which are expressive of lofty passion. Much more freedom does Horace allow himself in his satiric Hexameter. Moreover, many other poets (among the Romans) are accustomed to place monosyllabic Conjunctions or Prepositions in the caesura of the Hexameter, especially when elision occurs, as Vergil: —

> si genus huma*num et* mortalia temnitis arma.

The Greeks are much stricter in this respect, and a verse like the following (Il. I. 53) occurs but seldom: —

> ἐννῆμαρ μὲν ἀνὰ στρατὸν ᾤχετο κῆλα θεοῖο.

In the tragedians two verses like the following from Sophocles are rare: —

> κακὸν δὲ κἂν ἐν | ἡμέρᾳ γνοίης μιᾷ.

Therefore words like μέν, δέ, γάρ, οὖν, *enim, autem, vero*, which do not stand at the beginning of the sentence, are not usually found at the beginning of the verse.

Since languages, with increasing age, always pay more regard to logic, in the poets since the Christian era it is the rule that the end of a Strophe like the Elegiac Distich shall coincide with a full stop; and these poets also, even the Romans, — at least at the end of the verse, — avoid harsh discords between the end of a metrical series and the punctuation or logical connection.

9. Rhyme. Alliteration.

In order to emphasize words connected or related to each other by a similar sound, and because this sounded well to them, the Greeks and Romans often placed in the caesura and at the end of the verse words having a similar ending (rhyme, *homoeoteleuton*), especially a noun and adjective, or appositive, so that usually the last one, but sometimes the last two, syllables of each word had the same sound. Thus Homer:—

ἔσπετε νῦν μοι Μοῦσαι, Ὀλύμπια δώματ' ἔχουσαι.

Ovid:—
quot caelum *stellas*, tot habet tua Roma *puellas*.

Especially frequent is this assonance in the caesura and at the end of the verse of the dactylic Pentameter and the asclepiadeus minor, *e.g.*:—

et teneat cul*ti* jugera multa so*li*
terrarum domi*nos* evehit ad de*os*.

The laws of Rhyme in later poetry have been developed from this usage.

The same purpose is served by *Alliteration; i.e.* a similar beginning, consisting of one or even two letters, of two or more words which follow each other.

Among the Romans Alliteration appears frequently from the earliest time until Lucretius. Later, under the influence of the Greeks, who, with the exception of the comedians, were not fond of it, few instances occur, and these for the most part in single formulas, as *pater patriæ*, *more modoque*, etc., or in very artificial verses; in Vergil occasionally, in imitation of Ennius.[1]

[1] The relative merits and present relation of Greek and Roman versification are discussed in the Introduction.

SECOND SECTION.

ON PECULIARITIES OF THE FOOT.

10. Synapheia.

The last syllable of every verse can be, as has been already said, either long or short. Yet the old poets were fond of ending verses, especially those closing with a thesis or a trochee, with a long syllable or one ending with a consonant.

When several verses are joined together into one system by *Synapheia*,—that is, if the metre runs without break through the pauses of the verses to the end,—elision and the division of a word can occur at the end of every verse except the last. Hiatus and Syllaba Anceps, however, are not allowed. Especially frequent is Synapheia in Ionici *a minori*, Glyconics, and Anapæsts. Horace has Synapheia, but without elision and division of a word, in Od. III. 12; sometimes also in his other lyrical measures the same thing is found.

11. Resolution of Thesis and Arsis.

The Thesis of the dactylic verse, and of the logaœdic verse also in Ionic, Æolic, and Roman poetry, cannot be resolved. The Arsis in verses which have more than three feet can be replaced at pleasure by a long syllable.

The Arsis of the anapæst can always be replaced by a long syllable.

Resolution of Thesis and Arsis.

In anapæstic, iambic, and trochaic metres the Thesis, except the last, can always be replaced by a pyrrhic.

From this must be excepted iambic and trochaic verses ending with a spondee, as well as logaœdic metres; but this, too, apart from the Doric lyric poetry and the lyric passages of the drama. Further, the shorter an iambic and trochaic measure is, the less often does Resolution occur.

Wherever in iambic metre the spondee is allowed, it is occasionally replaced by an anapæst. This license is, however, found but seldom in the best poets, as the Greek tragedians and Horace. The Greeks allow the dactyl for the spondee in trochaic verse only in proper names.

Since the end of the verse, which in the Hexameter consists of two feet, in the longer iambic and trochaic measures, as well as in the Parœmiac, of one and a half feet, must be preserved in its original purity, we seldom find a spondee in the next to the last foot of the Hexameter or Parœmiac, or a Resolution of the next to the last Thesis in iambic or catalectic trochaic verse.

THIRD SECTION.

DESCRIPTION OF THE MOST IMPORTANT METRES, STROPHES, AND SYSTEMS.

12. Dactylic Metres.

(1) The Dactylic Hexameter [Homer and Hesiod][1]:—

The Hexameter was, in the Golden Age of antiquity, the only metre used for Epic poetry (*versus heroicus*), and for the responses of the oracles (*versus Pythius*). It was also the usual metre for Didactic and Bucolic poetry, and for Satire from Horace on; but it was seldom used in Epigrams other than those of folk-poetry. The tragedians employ it in some places, in especially solemn passages, and it occurs often in the strophes of Archilochus and Horace.

By the variety of its rhythms and cæsuras it is equally adapted to the most different kinds of poetry. The best Hexameters are those which are made up of three dactyls, and the spondees so arranged that the dactyls fall in the first, second, and fifth feet, as in Vergil:—

> arma virumque cano, Troiaeque primus ab oris.

[1] The name added to each metre in brackets indicates the poet by whom it was first used or through whom it first became known.

For too many dactyls make the rhythm too variable and restless; too many spondees make it stiff and clumsy. Hexameters made up of spondees only do not occur in the poets considered in this book, Homer not excepted (the readings in Od. XXI. 15; XXII. 175 are corrupt).

As would be expected from the flexibility of the language, among the Greeks the dactyl preponderates, so that its frequency of occurrence relatively to the spondee is as four to two.

Homer, and oftener Vergil, employ the different feet for verse-painting, according as the meaning demands more rapidity or slowness of rhythm. Thus in the well-known lines (Od. XI. 598; Æn. VIII. 596; Georg. IV. 174):—

> αὖτις ἔπειτα πέδονδε κυλίνδετο λᾶας ἀναιδής.
>
> quadrupedante putrem sonitu quatit ungula campum.
>
> illi inter sese magna vi bracchia tollunt.

Compare also the description of the storm (Æn. I. 81–91; 102–123).

In the fifth foot, especially in Latin, we do not often find the spondee (*versus spondiazon*), particularly in the Distich. In the Satires and Epistles of Horace it occurs only once (Ep. II. 3, 467).

If a spondee occurs in the fifth foot, a dactyl usually stands in the fourth.

The best and usual cæsura is the Penthemimeral, after the third Thesis:—

> μῆνιν ἄειδε, θεά. | Πηληιάδεω Ἀχιλῆος.
>
> arma virumque cano | Troiaeque primus ab oris.

Not less frequent in Homer and most of the Greek poets, much more frequent in Nonnus, is the τομὴ κατὰ τρίτον τροχαῖον (*i.e.* after the second syllable of the third dactyl) : —

ἄνδρα μοι ἔννεπε, Μοῦσα, | πολύτροπον, ὃς μάλα πολλά.

On the other hand, this occurs but seldom among the Romans. With them the caesura which occurs most frequently after the Penthemimeral is the Hephthemimeral, which is rare in Greek (*Æn.* I. 251) : —

navibus infandum! amissis | unius ob iram.

In Latin the Penthemimeral Caesura is by far the most frequent, especially so in the Distich, and in general in the most polished poetry.

Every Hexameter verse which has not one of these caesuras is faulty, and such do not occur in the poets considered in this book (the very few examples to the contrary are wholly corrupt readings).

In addition to the Penthemimeral Caesura and the τομὴ κατὰ τρίτον τροχαῖον, the so-called *Bucolic* Caesura (*i.e.* the caesura especially used in Bucolic poetry) after the fourth dactyl occurs, but only in Greek (Il. XXIII. 549 ; Od. I. 1) : —

ἔστι τοι ἐν κλισίῃ | χρυσὸς πολύς, | ἔστι δὲ χαλκός.

ἄνδρα μοι ἔννεπε, Μοῦσα, | πολύτροπον, | ὃς μάλα πολλά.

In cases where such verses occur in Latin, as Bucol. 10, 11, it is to be assumed that there is no caesura at all.

As the simple Hephthemimeral Caesura divides the verse into two unequal parts, there is frequently found both in Greek and Latin, as a sort of support, the Trithemimeral Caesura (after the second Thesis). So Il. I. 145 : — ·

ἢ Αἴας | ἢ Ἰδομενεὺς | ἢ δῖος Ὀδυσσεύς.

Dactylic Metres. 53

When the end of a word falls both in the second syllable of the third foot and in the fourth Thesis, in the Greek Hexameter the τομὴ κατὰ τρίτον τροχαῖον is employed, and in Latin the Hepthemimeral Cæsura, without regard to the punctuation (Od. IV. 126; Æn. IV. 582):—

> Ἀλκάνδρῃ Πολύβοιο | δάμαρ, ὃς ἔναι' ἐνὶ Θήβῃς.
> litora deseruere. latet | sub classibus aequor.

The Hephthemimeral Cæsura in Latin is most commonly found when at the same time the Trithemimeral occurs, and there is the end of a word in the third trochee:—

> infandum | regina jubes | renovare dolorem.

In this place, as at the end of the verse, too long words were avoided.

Finally, wherever in Latin Hexameter a word ends with the third Thesis, and after the fourth a decided stop occurs, the Hephthemimeral may be regarded as the proper cæsura:—

> oscula libavit natae ; | dehinc talia fatur.

When a word ends in the third trochee, a word ending also in the second or fourth trochee is not good, although in one case Horace has allowed himself both in one line:—

> dignum mente domoque | legentis honesta Neronis.

In a case like this when the Trithemimeral Cæsura does not occur, the best Latin poets are accustomed to unite the second and third feet in one word:—

> Mnesthea Sergestumque vocat | fortemque Serestum.

The Greeks in general very seldom place a trochaic word in the fourth foot, doubtless because they employ a trochee in the third foot so frequently.

Metres, Strophes, and Systems.

(2) The Pentameter (Callinus and Archilochus) is made up by doubling the first half of the Hexameter, which has the Penthemimeral Cæsura, though the spondee is allowed only in the first half:—

$$-\smile-\smile-\mid-\cup\cup-\cup\cup-$$

The most pleasing effect is produced when a spondee occurs only in the second foot:—

    et tene*at* cu*l*ti jugera multa soli.

The cæsura occurs always after the third Thesis.

The Distich is made up by the combination of the Pentameter (which almost never occurs alone) and the Hexameter.

$$-\smile-\smile-\mid\smile-\smile-\overset{\frown}{\smile}-\cup$$
$$-\smile-\smile-\mid-\cup\cup-\cup\cup-$$

(3) The Tetrameter (Archilochus):—

$$-\smile-\smile-\mid\smile-\cup\cup$$

This metre is employed by Horace and Archilochus in asynartete verse with a following trochaic Tripody. The last syllable is always short in Horace, but not in Archilochus. This verse also occurs independently in Greek and Roman lyrical poetry, in which case the dactyl greatly preponderates. The cæsura is the Penthemimeral.

(4) Tetrameter Catalectic *in disyllabum* (Archilochus):—

$$-\smile-\smile-\cup\cup-\cup$$

In Horace this is a part of the epodic and lyrical strophes. Only once (I. 28, 2) is a spondee found in the third foot, and then in a proper name.

(5) Trimeter Catalectic *in syllabam* (Archilochus): —

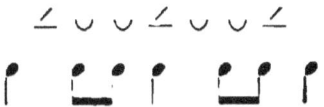

In Horace combined with the heroic Hexameter in the Odes. Elsewhere in the Epodes it is combined with the Iambic Dimeter into asynartete verse.

(6) Dimeter Catalectic *in dissyllabum, versus adonius* (Sappho): —

∠ ∪ ∪ ∠ ∪

This forms the close of the Sapphic Strophe.

13. Anapæstic Metres.

These do not occur in the Latin authors considered here, but frequently in the Greek dramatists.

(7) Anapæstic Dimeter: —

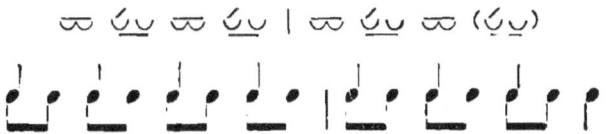

In place of an anapæst the spondee, dactyl, and proceleusmatic are allowed.

The poets usually avoid the proceleusmatic, as well for one foot as for the Thesis and Arsis of two successive feet, although cases are found where three proceleusmatics follow each other: —

∪ ∪ ◡́ ∪   ∪ ∪ ◡́ ∪   ∪ ∪ ◡́ ∪   ∪ ∪ ─́

The following form is usual: —

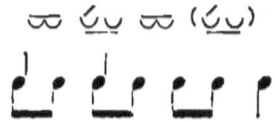

In solemn and mournful poetry, as in the marching hymns of the Spartans, the spondee was employed by preference.

The caesura after the first Dipody is not always observed.

(8) Anapæstic Monometer: —

∞ ◡́∪ ∞ (◡́∪)

This measure is often inserted in Anapæstic Systems.

Since the Anapæstic verse is employed in systems with Synapheia, Hiatus and Syllaba Anceps are only allowed at the end where there is a change of person, and more rarely at a stop. Elision and Resolution of the last Thesis are allowed. Notwithstanding the Synapheia, however, Dimeters and Monometers generally end with a complete word.

(9) The close of the Anapæstic System is usually formed by an Anapæstic Dimeter Catalectic (*versus paroemiacus*): —

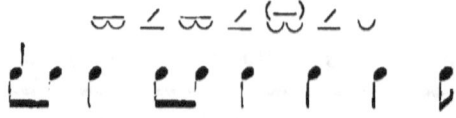

The rule is that this measure should have the form of the second half of the Hexameter after the Penthemimeral Cæsura. Hence it is rare that the Theses (especially the last) are resolved, or a spondee placed in the next to the last foot.

14. Iambic Metres.

(10) Iambic Trimeter *versus senarius* (Archilochus) : —

(a)   ⏑ –́ ⏑ –́ ⏑ –́ ⏑ –́ ⏑ –́ ⏑ –́

without Resolution or spondees. In Horace used with the dactylic Hexameter.

(b)   –̰ ⏑⏑́ ⏑ ⏑⏑́ –̰ ⏑⏑́ ⏑ ⏑⏑́ –̰ ⏑ (⏑⏑́) ⏑ –́

For Phædrus' Iambics, see below.

This is the most frequently used verse in the dialogue of Tragedy and Comedy and in the Epodes of Horace, and occasionally employed in other poetry, especially satirical and sarcastic. It is the favorite and most beautiful metre after the Dactylic Hexameter.

Spondees are particularly numerous in the Trimeter of Tragedy, especially in Æschylus. In general, here and in what follows, we are concerned only with the Iambic and Trochaic verses of the dialogue, not with those of the lyrical passages, which have their own peculiar licenses in Resolution, Cæsura, etc. Resolution of the Thesis occurs rarely in Archilochus, and is confined to the first syllable of words.

In Æschylus and the older plays of Sophocles, Resolution of the Thesis in the second, third, fourth, or fifth foot occurred more rarely, and then generally in the beginning of words of three or more syllables; less frequently in the case of dissyllabic words except prepositions, or monosyllables which belong closely to the following word beginning with a short syllable, *e.g.* the article. Euripides, in whose poetry Resolution is oftenest found, allows himself to unite a short monosyllable with a following short syllable when both words do not belong together.

In words of four or more syllables in the second and fifth feet inclusive, Resolution through the two last syllables occurs, but in Euripides only through the middle syllables. In the first foot it is naturally the second and third syllables of a word of three or more syllables which are employed in a Resolution of the Thesis. Yet Sophocles and chiefly Euripides (even Æschylus when the first foot is a dactyl) allow the verse to begin with a monosyllable. A Resolution is not allowed when its first syllable forms the close of a polysyllabic word.

Resolution occurs most frequently in the third Thesis (after the cæsura) and in the first, most rarely in the fifth. A dactyl instead of a spondee occurs only in the first and third feet.

Æschylus has seldom two cases of Resolution in one verse; Euripides has not seldom even three.

Horace never divides a Resolution into two words, and out of the first foot, he uses it only twice in a dissyllable (Ep. 2, 23; 5, 87). A word consisting of three short syllables in Latin is used in the place of a trochee, never in place of an iambus, as is customary in Greek. Therefore in Latin verse it is possible to scan gĕnĕră, never gĕnĕrā.

In the same way the two last short syllables in words of more than three syllables, *e.g.* materĭă, are not used in a Resolution. Horace does not even use in this way the last syllables of a dactylic word like rŏbŏră. He never resolves the fifth Thesis; the tribrach occurs most frequently in the second foot, and he rarely has two Resolutions in one verse, almost never three (cf. Ep. 17, 12).

The anapæst can stand instead of the spondee in the first foot in tragedy, and for this a word of three or more syllables is generally used. Elsewhere the anapæst is allowed only in proper names, but (in such names) in all feet except the last.

Horace has an anapæst twice in the first foot, three times in the fifth (Ep. 2, 35; 65; 3, 35; 5, 79; 11, 23), always in a word of at least three syllables.

The Arsis of an anapæst can never be formed by the two last syllables of a word of more than two syllables, or by the final of a polysyllable and the first syllable of the following word. The proceleusmatic is not allowed.

As in the Dactylic Hexameter, the most usual cæsura is the Penthemimeral after the third Arsis:—

$$\cup - \cup - \cup\ |\ - \cup - \cup - \cup -$$
ibis Liburnis | inter alta navium;

Next the Hephthemimeral after the fourth Arsis:—

$$\cup - \cup - \cup - \cup\ |\ - \cup - \cup -$$
nam qualis aut Molossus | aut fulvus Laco.

The Penthemimeral Cæsura preponderates in Euripides more than in Æschylus and Sophocles, and most of all in Horace.

Since the Hephthemimeral Cæsura divides the verse too unequally, it is especially used when the second foot ends with the end of a word:—

nam qual*is aut* Molossus aut fulvus Laco;

or when the second and third trochees of the verse are formed by one word:—

quae sidera *excantata* voce Thessala.

Finally, when the end of a word comes after the second trochee, and a stop after the third, the Hephthemimeral Cæsura is to be assumed:—

quid dixit aut quid tacuit? | o rebus meis.

The rules of the Hephthemimeral Cæsura in the dactylic Hexameter are quite similar (cf. **12**).

A Trimeter without either the Penthemimeral or Hephthemimeral Cæsura is faulty. Such verses do occur in the tragedies, but not in Horace. In such cases a word usually ends with the third foot.

Finally, it is to be noticed that when the fifth foot is a spondee, the tragedians are not accustomed to use the final of a polysyllabic word as its Arsis, except when an enclitic follows, or a monosyllable closely connected with the preceding word, as *e.g.*:—

σπεύδωμεν, ἐγκονῶμεν· ἡγοῦ μοι, γερον.

οἷόν τέ μοι τάσδ᾽ ἐστί. θνητοῖς γὰρ γέρα.

Otherwise the last cretic would be too forcibly separated from the rest of the verse. Horace has observed this rule only in Ep. 17.

IAMBICS OF PHÆDRUS.

Phædrus allows the spondee or the anapæst in every foot except the last.

In the fifth foot the spondee or anapæst predominate; the iambus is admitted principally when a four-syllabled word stands at the end of the line:—

ranae vagantes liberis *paludibus*.

In no case does a verse close with two iambic words.

The tribrach occurs only in the second, third, and fourth feet; the dactyl generally in the first, third, and fourth. The Resolution of the Thesis follows in other respects the same rules as in Horace, except that pyrrhic words are more frequently employed, very rarely monosyllables, which are usually closely connected with the following short syllable: —

> calumniator *ăb ŏve* cum peteret canis.

The verse in app. 10, 10, is an isolated case and probably to be emended: —

> non ut labores facio, *sed ut* istum domes.

If the fifth Thesis is resolved, a four-syllabled word at least must stand at the end of the verse. The verses V. 7, 22; app. 9, 6, hardly constitute an exception.

The anapæst stands everywhere in place of the spondee; the two never follow each other immediately. Except in the first foot and (very seldom) in the fifth (III. 10, 4; 14, 11; app. 19, 3; 30, 10), Phædrus follows exactly the same rules as Horace for the anapæst.

In the first foot the Arsis is almost always formed by a dissyllable or the beginning of a polysyllable. The proceleusmatic occurs only in the first foot; in such wise that the Arsis always forms a word for itself, and the Thesis does the same, or at least forms the pyrrhic beginning of a word, *e.g.*: —

> *ita caput* ad nostrum furor illorum pertinet.
> *itaque hodie* nec lucernam de flamma deum.

The cæsura is exclusively the Penthemimeral or (more rarely) the Hephthemimeral.

(11) Catalectic Trimeter (Archilochus): —

$$\cup \perp \cup \perp \cup \mid \perp \cup \perp \cup \perp \cup$$

This is used by Horace in the Odes. Resolution of the Thesis and the anapæst are not allowed; for the reading in II. 18, 34, is certainly corrupt. The cæsura is always the Penthemimeral.

(12) Iambic Dimeter Hypercatalectic (Alcæus):—

$$(\smile) \perp \smile \perp - \perp \smile \perp \smile$$

This is used by Alcæus and Horace as the third verse of the Alcaic and logaœdic strophe, and therefore the Thesis is never resolved. This verse occurs only in Horace in the form given above. In Alcæus the first and fifth syllables can be either long or short. The Anacrusis is generally long in the first three books of Horace's Odes, and always long in the fourth.

(13) Iambic Dimeter (Archilochus):—

$$\smile \perp \smile \perp \smile \perp \smile \perp$$

Used by Archilochus and Horace as the second verse of the Epode, and in asynartete verses; by the other poets also as a separate measure.

An iambus seldom occurs in the third foot. Resolution occurs in Horace only twice, once in the first foot, and once in order to produce a rhythmical picture (Ep. 15, 24; 2, 62).

15. Trochaic Metres.

(14) Trochaic Tetrameter Catalectic (Archilochus):—

Trochaic Metres.

This metre is common in the Greek and Latin drama, and resembles closely the Iambic Trimeter, except that it is much more strictly formed in the Greek tragedy. Resolution of the Thesis takes place most frequently in the uneven feet and in the first half of the verse — very seldom in the seventh Thesis.

In resolving the Arsis, Euripides first dared to make use of dissyllabic words, or the penultimate and final syllables of trisyllables. Very rarely do two monosyllables occur in the Resolution, if they are not closely connected with a following short syllable. The dactyl in place of the spondee is not allowed. The caesura falls in tragedy without exception after the second dipody (Æsch. Pers. 164; Soph. Philoct. 1402 are corrupt readings).

If the sixth foot is a spondee, it cannot be a dissyllable or the end of a polysyllable.

(15) Trochaic Dimeter Catalectic : —

$$-\cup-\cup-\cup-$$

This form occurs in Horace, Od. II. 18; also frequently in the lyrical parts of tragedy, and usually just as here given.

(16) Trochaic Tripody, *versus ithyphallicus* (Archilochus) : —

$$-\cup-\cup-\cup$$

Used by Archilochus and Horace in asynartete verses with a preceding Dactylic Tetrameter.

16. Ionici a Minori.

(17) Decameter (Alcæus):—

∪∪––∪∪––∪∪––∪∪––|
∪∪––∪∪––∪∪––∪∪––|∪∪––∪∪––

This is used by Horace, in imitation of Alcæus, in the Odes. The cæsura falls after the fourth and eighth feet.

17. Logaœdic Metres.

(18) Glyconic (Sappho, Anacreon); in Horace in the following form:—

– – – ∪ ∪ – ∪ –

The Glyconic metre was originally a logaœdic series

– ∪ ∪ – ∪ –

with a two-syllable Basis of any convenient quantity.

This license belonged also to the Pherecratean and Asclepiadean verses, which were derived from the Glyconic. Catullus, the predecessor of Horace, used as the Basis of the Glyconic and Pherecratean, generally the trochee, more rarely the spondee and iambus. Horace, however, uses the spondee exclusively as the Basis of all these verses, as Catullus does in his Asclepiadean verses.

The tragedians allow in the Basis of the Glyconic verse beside the trochee, spondee, iambus, and pyrrhic, also the tribrach, and Euripides even admits the anapæst.

Sophocles, and much more frequently Euripides, created very varied forms of the Glyconic (*glyconei polyschematisti*) by means of a displacement of the dactyl and other licenses.

(19) Pherecratean (Sappho, Anacreon) : —

$$\acute{-}\,^{(\geq)}\,\acute{-}\,\cup\,\cup\,\acute{-}\,^{(\geq)}$$

This metre is not used alone, but only in combination with Glyconic and Asclepiadean verses.

(20) Lesser Asclepiadean (Alcæus) : —

$$\acute{-}\,^{(\geq)}\,\acute{-}\,\cup\,\cup\,\acute{-}\,|\,\_\,\cup\,\cup\,\_\,\cup\,\_$$

This verse is formed by the insertion of one choriambus after the Basis, as the following verse is formed by the insertion of two.

The cæsura after the sixth foot is always observed by Horace, though sometimes neglected by Alcæus.

(21) Greater Asclepiadean, dodecasyllabic (Alcæus) : —

$$\acute{-}\,\_\,\acute{-}\,\cup\,\cup\,\acute{-}\,|\,\acute{-}\,\cup\,\cup\,\acute{-}\,|\,\acute{-}\,\cup\,\cup\,\acute{-}\,\cup\,\acute{-}$$

Cf. No. 20. The cæsura after the sixth and tenth syllables is often neglected by Sappho, Alcæus, and Catullus, never by Horace.

(22) Greater Sapphic (Sappho) : —

$$\acute{-}\,\cup\,\acute{-}\,\_\,\acute{-}\,|\,\cup\,\cup\,\acute{-}\,\cup\,\acute{-}\,\cup$$

Two trochaic dipodies, divided by a dactyl. Horace employs always a spondee in place of the second trochee. In Sappho the fourth syllable is either long or short, and Catullus has sometimes a short syllable here. The cæsura is generally after the third Thesis, occasionally (especially in the fourth book of the Odes and the Carm. Sacc.) after the trochee of the third foot. This cæsura is often neglected by Sappho — by Catullus only twice.

(23) Lesser Sapphic, aristophaneus (Sappho):—

$$-\cup\cup-\cup-\cup$$

(24) The so-called Sapphic verse of fifteen syllables is formed by a combination from the beginning and end of the Greater Sapphic, but this occurs first in Horace:—

$$-\cup--\,-\mid\cup\cup-\mid-\cup\cup-\cup-\cup$$

The fifth and eighth syllables are always final.

(25) Alcaic Hendecasyllabic (Alcæus):—

$$(\cup)-\cup-\,-\mid-\cup\cup-\cup-$$

Logaœdic Metre with Anacrusis, which is common in Alcæus. In Horace the Anacrusis is generally long in the first three books of Odes and always so in the fourth. Alcæus has often the original trochee instead of the spondee before the cæsura. The cæsura is sometimes neglected by Alcæus, but only twice by Horace (I. 37, 14; IV. 14, 17, though these verses are probably corrupt).

(26) Alcaic Decasyllabic (Alcæus):—

$$-\cup\cup-\cup\cup-\cup-\cup$$

This forms the close of the Alcaic Strophe.

18. Asynartete Verse (Mixed Measures).

(27) Greater Archilochian (Archilochus):—

$$-\overline{\cup}-\overline{\cup}-\mid\overline{\cup}-\cup\cup\mid-\cup-\cup-\cup$$

A combination of the Dactylic Tetrameter (No. 3) and the Versus Ithyphallicus (No. 16).

(28) Elegiambic (Archilochus): —

$$\acute{-}\cup\cup\acute{-}\cup\cup\acute{-}\,|\,\overline{\cup}\,\acute{-}\cup\acute{-}\,\overline{\cup}\,\acute{-}\cup\acute{-}$$

A combination of the Dactylic Trimeter Catalectic (No. 5) and the Iambic Dimeter (No. 13). Short syllables and Hiatus occur in the third Thesis.

(29) Iambelegiac: —

$$\overline{\cup}\,\acute{-}\cup\acute{-}\,\overline{\cup}\,\acute{-}\cup\acute{-}\,|\,\acute{-}\cup\cup\acute{-}\cup\cup\acute{-}$$

A combination like the preceding, but with the order of the measures reversed. This verse, which possesses much force and liveliness because of the transition from the Iambic to the Dactylic measure, is first found in Horace. A short syllable often occurs in the fourth Thesis.

19. The Elegiac Distich (Callinus, Archilochus).

$$\acute{-}\,\overline{\cup\cup}\,\acute{-}\,\overline{\cup\cup}\,\acute{-}\,|\,\overline{\cup\cup}\,\acute{-}\,\overline{\cup\cup}\,\acute{-}\,\overset{(\overline{\cup})}{\overline{\cup\cup}}\,\acute{-}\cup$$
$$\acute{-}\,\overline{\cup\cup}\,\acute{-}\,\overline{\cup\cup}\,\acute{-}\,|\,\acute{-}\cup\cup\acute{-}\cup\cup\acute{-}$$

This is the oldest and most beautiful verse-system of the Greeks; a combination of the Dactylic Hexameter and Pentameter (Nos. 1 and 2). It was employed mostly in Epigram and Elegy. It is somewhat less appropriate for Didactic Poetry, though used by Ovid in the *Fasti* and by Propertius.

It was a favorite metre among the Greeks, and still more so among the Romans, who developed it with marvellous artistic skill.

20. The Lyric Strophes of Horace.[1]

These Lyric Strophes of Horace are all composed of four lines, perhaps in imitation of Alcæus, but not of Archilochus.

---

[1] Here are given, just as in the case of the Distich, the most usual schemes of the individual verses. For everything else, see the discussion in the preceding section.

At the close of single verses Syllaba Anceps (sometimes with a final consonant) often occurs, more rarely Hiatus. Sometimes at the ends of the first three verses we find a word divided or Elision. In both these cases the final syllable is always long.

(1) Alcaic Strophe (Alcæus):—

$$(\smile)\ \angle \smile \angle \_ \ |\ \angle \smile \smile \angle \smile \angle$$
$$(\smile)\ \angle \smile \angle \_ \ |\ \angle \smile \smile \angle \smile \angle$$
$$(\smile)\ \angle \smile \angle \_ \ \ \angle \smile \angle \smile$$
$$\angle \smile \smile \angle \ \ \smile \smile \angle \smile \angle \smile$$

This is made up of the Alcaic Hendecasyllabic (No. 25), the Enneasyllabic (12), and the Decasyllabic (26), and is characterized by force and energy. Therefore it is Horace's favorite metre, and employed by him especially in Odes of political and moral content, though also in those treating of erotic and convivial subjects. It is the metre of 37 Odes: I. 9. 16. 17. 26. 27. 29. 31. 34. 35. 37; II. 1. 3. 5. 7. 9. 11. 13–15. 17. 19. 20; III. 1–6. 17. 21. 23. 26. 29; IV. 4. 9. 14. 15.

Elision at the end of the verse occurs in II. 3. 27; III. 29. 35.

(2) Sapphic Strophe (Sappho):—

$$\angle \smile \angle \_ \angle \ |\ \smile \smile \angle \smile \angle \smile$$
$$\angle \smile \angle \_ \angle \ |\ \smile \smile \angle \smile \angle \smile$$
$$\angle \smile \angle \_ \angle \ |\ \smile \smile \angle \smile \angle \smile$$
$$\angle \smile \smile \angle \smile$$

Made up of the Sapphic Hendecasyllabic (22) and the Adonic (6). This strophe has more grace and tenderness than force and energy. Hence it would, perhaps, have been better if Horace had not used it so often in Odes written in lofty style. It occurs in 26 Odes: I. 2. 10. 12.

Lyric Strophes of Horace. 69

20. 22. 25. 30. 32. 38; II. 2. 4. 6. 8. 10. 16; III. 8. 11. 14. 18. 20. 22. 27; IV. 2. 6. 11; Carm. Saec.

Elision at the end of a verse occurs in II. 2, 18; 16, 34; IV. 2, 22; 23; Carm. Saec. 47. The division of a word, in each case at the end of the third verse, occurs four times: I. 2, 19; 25, 11; II. 16, 7; III. 27, 59.

(3) Second Sapphic Strophe:—

$$-\cup\cup-\cup-\cup$$
$$-\cup-\_- \mid \cup\cup- \mid -\cup\cup-\cup-\cup$$

Made up of the Lesser Sapphic (23) and the so-called fifteen-syllabled Sapphic (24). 1, 8.

(4) First Asclepiadean Strophe:—

$$-\_-\cup\cup- \mid -\cup\cup-\cup-$$

Made up of the Lesser Asclepiadean repeated (20). I. 1; III. 30; IV. 8.

(5) Second Asclepiadean Strophe:—

$$-\_-\cup\cup- \mid -\cup\cup-\cup-$$
$$-\_-\cup\cup- \mid -\cup\cup-\cup-$$
$$-\_-\cup\cup- \mid -\cup\cup-\cup-$$
$$-\_-\cup\cup-\cup\_$$

Made up of the Lesser Asclepiadean (20) and the Glyconic (18). The metre of nine Odes: I. 6. 15. 24. 33; II. 12; III. 10. 16; IV. 5. 12.

(6) Third Asclepiadean Strophe:—

$$-\_-\cup\cup- \mid -\cup\cup-\cup-$$
$$-\_-\cup\cup- \mid -\cup\cup-\cup-$$
$$-\_-\cup\cup-\cup$$
$$-\_-\cup\cup-\cup-$$

Made up of the Lesser Asclepiadean (20), the Phere-

cratean (19) and the Glyconic (18). Occurs in seven
Odes: I. 5. 14. 21. 23; III. 7. 13; IV. 13.

(7) Fourth Asclepiadean Strophe:—

$$\acute{-}-\acute{-}\cup\cup\acute{-}\cup\acute{-}$$
$$\acute{-}-\acute{-}\cup\cup\acute{-}\,|\,\acute{-}\cup\cup\acute{-}\cup\acute{-}$$
$$\acute{-}-\acute{-}\cup\cup\acute{-}\cup\acute{-}$$
$$\acute{-}-\acute{-}\cup\cup\acute{-}\,|\,\acute{-}\cup\cup\acute{-}\cup\acute{-}$$

Made up of the Glyconic (18) and the Lesser Asclepiadean (20). This is the metre of 12 Odes: I. 3. 13. 19. 36; III. 9. 15. 19. 24. 25. 28; IV. 1. 3. Elision at the end of a verse occurs in IV. 1. 35.

(8) Fifth Asclepiadean Strophe (used by Sappho and Catullus, but in couplets):—

$$\acute{-}-\acute{-}\cup\cup\acute{-}\,|\,-\cup\cup\acute{-}\,|\,\acute{-}\cup\cup\acute{-}\cup\acute{-}$$

Made up of Greater Asclepiadean verses (21). I. 11. 18; IV. 10.

(9) First Archilochian Strophe:—

$$\acute{-}\,\overline{\cup}\,\acute{-}\,\overline{\cup}\,\acute{-}\,|\,\overline{\cup}\,\acute{-}\,\overline{\cup}\,\acute{-}\,\cup\cup\acute{-}\cup$$
$$\acute{-}\cup\cup\acute{-}\cup\cup\acute{-}$$
$$\acute{-}\,\overline{\cup}\,\acute{-}\,\overline{\cup}\,\acute{-}\,|\,\overline{\cup}\,\acute{-}\,\overline{\cup}\,\acute{-}\,\cup\cup\acute{-}\cup$$
$$\acute{-}\cup\cup\acute{-}\cup\cup\acute{-}$$

Made up of the Dactylic Hexameter (1) and Catalectic Trimeter (5). IV. 7.

(10) Second Archilochian Strophe:—

$$\acute{-}\,\overline{\cup}\,\acute{-}\,\overline{\cup}\,\acute{-}\,|\,\overline{\cup}\,\acute{-}\,\overline{\cup}\,\acute{-}\,(\overset{\smile}{\smile})\,\acute{-}\cup$$
$$\acute{-}\,\overline{\cup}\,\acute{-}\,\overline{\cup}\,\acute{-}\,(\overset{\smile}{\smile})\,\acute{-}\cup$$
$$\acute{-}\,\overline{\cup}\,\acute{-}\,\overline{\cup}\,\acute{-}\,|\,\overline{\cup}\,\acute{-}\,\overline{\cup}\,\acute{-}\,\cup\cup\acute{-}\cup$$
$$\acute{-}\,\overline{\cup}\,\acute{-}\,\overline{\cup}\,\acute{-}\,\cup\cup\acute{-}\cup$$

Made up of the Dactylic Hexameter (1) and the Catalectic Tetrameter (4). 1, 7, 28. Also used in Epode 12, but in couplets.

(11) Third Archilochian Strophe (used by Archilochus in couplets) :—

−⏕−⏕−|⏕−◡◡|−◡−◡−◡
×−◡−×|−◡−◡−◡
−⏕−⏕−|⏕−◡◡|−◡−◡−◡
×−◡−×|−◡−◡−◡

Made up of the Greater Archilochian (27) and the Iambic Trimeter Catalectic (11). I. 4.

(12) Hipponactean Strophe :—

−◡−◡−◡−
×−◡−×|−◡−◡−◡
−◡−◡−◡−
×−◡−×|−◡−◡−◡

A combination of the Trochaic Dimeter Catalectic (15) and the Iambic Trimeter Catalectic (11). II. 18.

(13) Strophe of Ionici a minori :—

◡◡−−◡◡−−◡◡−−◡◡−−|
◡◡−−◡◡−−◡◡−−◡◡−−|◡◡−−◡◡−−

Made up of the Ionicus a minori Decameter (17) (repeated). III. 12.

Syllaba Anceps and Hiatus are not allowed except at the close of the Strophe.

21. Epodic Systems.

The Epodes of Horace are written in couplets, except the last, which is made up of Iambic Trimeters κατὰ στίχον.

Metres, Strophes, and Systems.

(1) Iambic System (Archilochus):—

$$\cup \underline{\ }\cup \underline{\ }\cup \mid \underline{\ }\cup \underline{\ }\cup \underline{\ }\cup \underline{\ }$$
$$\cup \underline{\ }\cup \underline{\ }\cup \underline{\ }\cup \underline{\ }$$

Made up of the Iambic Trimeter (10*b*) and the Iambic Dimeter (13). Ep. 1–10.

(2) First Archilochian System:—

$$\cup (\overset{\smile}{\underline{\ }}) \cup \underline{\ }\cup \mid \underline{\ }\cup \underline{\ }\overset{(\smile)}{\cup} \underline{\ }\cup \underline{\ }$$
$$\underline{\ }\cup\cup \underline{\ }\cup\cup \underline{\ } \mid \cup \underline{\ }\cup \underline{\ }\cup \underline{\ }\cup \underline{\ }$$

Made up of the Iambic Trimeter (10*b*) and the Elegiambic (28). Ep. 11.

(3) Second Archilochian System:—

$$\underline{\ }\infty \underline{\ }\infty \underline{\ } \mid \infty \underline{\ }\infty \underline{\ }(\overset{\smile}{\smile}) \underline{\ }\cup$$
$$\cup \underline{\ }\cup \underline{\ }\cup \underline{\ }\cup \underline{\ } \mid \underline{\ }\cup\cup \underline{\ }\cup\cup \underline{\ }$$

Made up of the Dactylic Hexameter (1) and the Iambelegiac (29). Ep. 13.

(4) Third Archilochian System:—

$$\underline{\ }\infty \underline{\ }\infty \underline{\ } \mid \infty \underline{\ }\infty \underline{\ }\cup\cup \underline{\ }\cup$$
$$\underline{\ }\infty \underline{\ }\infty \underline{\ }\cup\cup \underline{\ }\cup$$

Made up of the Dactylic Hexameter (1) and the Dactylic Tetrameter Catalectic (4). Ep. 12. Cf. also Strophe 10 of the Lyrical Metres.

(5) First Pythiambic System:—

$$\underline{\ }\infty \underline{\ }\infty \underline{\ } \mid \infty \underline{\ }\infty \underline{\ }\cup\cup \underline{\ }\cup$$
$$\cup \underline{\ }\cup \underline{\ }\cup \underline{\ }\cup \underline{\ }$$

Made up of the Dactylic Hexameter (1) and the Iambic Dimeter (13). Ep. 14. 15.

(6) Second Pythiambic System: —

$$\angle \smile\smile \angle \smile\smile \angle\ |\ \smile\smile \angle \smile\smile \angle \overset{\smile}{\smile} \angle \cup$$
$$\cup \angle \cup \angle \cup\ |\ \angle \cup \angle \cup \angle \cup \angle$$

Made up of the Dactylic Hexameter (1) and the pure Iambic Trimeter (10a). Ep. 16.

FOURTH SECTION.

―――∽∘⁚∾⁚∘∾―――

ON METRICAL LICENSES.

22. Preface.

The structure of the verse is determined by fixed laws, which, however, are sometimes neglected or evaded.

Still such exceptions are almost never arbitrary in the classical writers; rather do they, too, fall under definite rules, which are of only less wide application than the general laws of the verse. They are, so to speak, dissonances resolved into a higher consonance.

23. Metrical Licenses.

The metrical licenses and peculiarities of the poets can be reduced to eight cases:—

(1) The beginning of every metrical series has greater freedom than the end of the series formed either by the caesura or the close of the verse.

(2) Long verses enjoy greater freedom than short; so long poems offer greater opportunity for metrical licenses than shorter ones which must be especially characterized by elegance and beauty of form.

(3) Variation of subject-matter often introduces variation of metrical laws, especially among the Greeks. Thus epic poetry, as well as didactic, satirical, and elegiac, has certain peculiar forms of the Hexameter. In the same

way, the lyric versification has its peculiarities, and that of comedy often differs widely from that of tragedy.

(4) Further, it is clear that the inventor of a metre, or one who introduces innovations therein, treats it more freely than later writers who follow the path which he has opened up. The Hexameter of Ennius differs widely from that of Vergil; the lyric measures of Horace from those of Seneca. In general, it is true that the more frequently any metre is used, the more exact is its structure.

(5) The later works of an author are usually more polished than the earlier. For instance, the Hexameters of Horace's Epistles are more carefully formed than those of the Satires.

(6) As the metrical art of the famous poets of antiquity continued to be the standard for those who came later, or at least exercised great influence on them, it is very important to observe what model of versification each poet has followed. The Hexameters of the post-Augustan poets vary according as they follow Vergil or Ovid.

(7) Frequently the metrical licenses of a verse can be explained by the occurrence in the verse of proper names, or (in Latin) of Greek words, especially immediately before such words; for proper names cannot be arbitrarily rewritten or altered. It is to be remembered, too, that the ancient poets employed these names much more frequently than those of modern times. Moreover, Greek words appear in Latin verse to justify of themselves, at the same time, the metrical licenses borrowed from the Greeks. In didactic poetry the so-called *termini technici*, in the Christian writers sacred words as *spiritus*, *ecclesia*, usually give rise to metrical licenses, for these words approach nearly to proper names. In the same class, too, fall sometimes

words of four or more syllables, as well as the most common pronouns, adverbs, prepositions and conjunctions, and certain fixed expressions like "ἢ οὔ," "ergo age," "quare age."

(8) Finally metrical licenses are not seldom occasioned by an impassioned movement of the language which shows itself in rhetorical figures, especially in the repetition of the same word (anaphora) or in antithesis.

It is often true that several of these reasons combine to explain a single case of metrical license.

In Greek poetry metrical licenses are much more frequent than in Latin, although there are cases where several of them occur in a single Latin Hexameter when some of the above-mentioned excuses are present. Thus the verse of Vergil: —

   Nereidum matri et Neptuno Aegaeo,

contains two cases of hiatus — a spondee in the fifth foot, and a violation of the rhythmical laws of this same foot.

FIFTH SECTION.

ON THE RHYTHMICAL STRUCTURE OF THE VERSE.

24. General Remarks.

(1) As poetry, at least in its higher forms, seeks to differentiate itself as widely as possible from the ordinary methods of expression in prose, the poets avoid allowing the rhythm of the verse to coincide with the prose accent of the words, as far as it is at all practicable. It is likewise considered improper to introduce a verse into prose.

The first law, then, is that there shall be the greatest possible difference between the metrical rhythm and the prose accent. This law naturally has the least force in those parts of the verse which admit the greatest freedom of structure, as at the beginning of a metrical series, at the beginning of the verse, or after the caesura, as *e.g.* in Vergil :—

litora, multum ille et terris jactatus et alto.

ipse hostis Teucros | *insigni* laude ferebat.

This law is further modified by the following rules.

(2) As the verse becomes in the first instance a work of art by the close and harmonious combination of the feet, it is not usual, at least in the longer verses, to allow single feet to consist of single words. Consequently the following Hexameter from Ennius is bad :—

sparsis hostis longis campus splendet et horret.

In order therefore that the verse may not fall apart, the individual feet must run into each other as much as possible, and this result is obtained most effectually by the greatest possible difference between the compass of the individual words and of the single feet.

(3) Finally, the end of every metrical series, be it at the caesura or at the end of the verse, must faithfully represent the rhythm of the foot with which it ends, e.g. the anapæstic rhythm at the Penthemimeral Cæsura of the Dactylic Hexameter, and the trochaic at the end of the whole verse.

Since it is the first law of ancient versification that the metrical rhythm shall differ as far as possible from the prose accent, it is considered less objectionable when, at the end of a metrical series, the original rhythm is violated in such a way that the poetical rhythm does not harmonize with the prose accent, than when the opposite is true. This can be observed in the rhythmical laws of the Hexameter.

At the cæsural pause, the end of the metrical series, the rhythm of which must be kept pure, consists of one foot; at the close of longer verses of one and a half or two feet, and at the close of shorter verses of one.

It is, however, clear that this rule is principally applicable to poetry written κατὰ στίχον, and to such systems as are not united by Synapheia, as e.g. the Dactylic Distich and the Iambic Epode. Where Synapheia can or must occur, and the single verses form properly only sections of a single metrically harmonious whole, violations of the rule in question are more frequent and more easily pardoned.

Above all, the occurrence of a monosyllable at the end of a metrical series is to be avoided, except where another monosyllable precedes, and this rule is so much the more to be observed, the longer the preceding word is and the greater the number of *moræ* that it has. Therefore the least unpleasant effect is produced where a pyrrhic word precedes the monosyllable. Hence the verses from Vergil are bad: —

> et cum *frigida mors* anima seduxerit artus.
>
> dat latus. insequitur cumulo praeruptus *aquae mons*.

The reason for this is that a monosyllable, on account of its small compass, has not the force necessary to draw towards itself a polysyllable, and the consequence is that in verses like those just quoted the end of the metrical series is separated.

25. Rhythmical Structure of the Hexameter and Pentameter.

We wish to explain more at length the above-mentioned laws in the case of some of the most common metres, since these are at the same time the most carefully formed, and to do this by illustration from the Latin poets — for they developed the single metres especially as regards rhythm more carefully than the Greeks, — remembering that nearly the same rhythmical laws are valid also for Greek poetry.

We consider first the Dactylic Hexameter.

First of all, it is plain that no word ending with a dactyl can stand in the second and third foot of the Hexameter, — still less a word ending in a spondee, since the spondee is not the original measure of this verse.

So we find only twice in Horace (Epist. I. 18, 52; II. 3, 41) a word ending with a dactyl in the third foot, and

not at all in the other poets considered here. Further
Vergil and Propertius (not Ovid and Tibullus) have
seldom in the second foot a word ending with a dactyl,
and never one ending with a spondee. In Horace in the
Epistles and Satires this occurrence is somewhat more
frequent. Hence the following lines cannot be recom-
mended in this respect : —

> et cum *frigida* mors anima seduxerit artus.
> per *conubia* nostra, per ince... os hymenaeos.

Still worse is this from Ennius : —

> ore *Cethegus* Marcu' Tuditano collega.

Less frequently do we find before the Penthemimeral
Cæsura a pyrrhic word followed by a monosyllable, as : —

> ille autem : *neque te* | Phœbi cortina fefellit.

it to find two or three monosyllables : —

> (..) quoties *et quae* | nobis Galatea locutast.
> simplicior *quis et est?* | qualem me saepe libenter.

It is usual at the se, nthemimeral Cæsura to find a word
ending with an .. ..., spondee, or iambus.

What has just been said holds also for the Hephthemimeral Cæsura. On the other hand, a dactylic word not
seldom forms the arsis of the Trithemimeral Cæsura, since
this lies in the first foot.

At the end of the sixth foot a monosyllable is allowed
only when the thesis is also a monosyllable : —

> at Boreae de part ..is cum fulminat *et cum*.

The thesis of the fifth fo... .. monosyllable if a
pyrrhic word or two monosyllables follow :

> nam neque Parnasi vobis juga, *nam neque* Pindi.
> cederet aut quarta socialiter. *hic et in* Acci.

Structure of Hexameter and Pentameter. 81

But a monosyllable is disagreeable in the fifth thesis if more than two syllables follows. In the same way the fifth thesis cannot be the end of a polysyllable, for in such a case this (thesis) becomes anapæstic through its close connection with the arsis of the fourth foot, while it is separated from the fifth arsis which belongs to it, by the end of the word. Consequently verses like the following seldom occur: —

> fixerit aeripedem cervam licet *aut Erymanthi*.
> tres Antenoridas Cererique *sacrum Polyphoeten*.

Finally, it is not usual to make the fifth and sixth feet out of one word of five syllables, as in Horace: —

> divisit medium fortissima *Tyndaridarum*.

The reason for this is that, in Latin, the two last syllables of such long words are usually inflectional or derivative endings, and the beginning a preposition or the like, and therefore have more sound than meaning, they seem feeble at the end of the verse which should close forcibly. It is for this cause and not for metrical reasons that they are avoided. In Greek, on the other hand, five-syllabled words are usually compounds of noun and verb, and not so empty of meaning as most Latin words of corresponding length. Hence there is far less reason for avoiding them.

It is usual to find in the fifth foot a word with dactylic ending, and in the sixth a dissyllable; or in the first case a word with trochaic ending, and in the second a trisyllable: —

> in nova fert animus — *is dicere formas*.
> insign— — *ot ad*ire *labores*.

But the second arsis of the fifth foot can be a monosyllable: —

> arma virumque cano, Troiae qui *primus ab oris*.

A monosyllable in the sixth foot preceded by a polysyllable occurs more than forty times in Vergil; in Ovid only eleven times. Vergil violates the rhythmical laws of the fifth foot about one hundred and twenty times; Ovid only eighty times. Many of the later writers are still more strict. Horace, on the other hand, is less strict in the Hexameters of the Satires and Epistles. The exceptions found in Vergil and Ovid are almost always occasioned by one of the reasons noted in Section 4.

Moreover, Vergil makes admirable use of discordant verse-endings in order to express by the rhythm itself what is dreadful, weird, or unexpected: —

> vertitur interea caelum et ruit Oceano nox.
> et nunc ille Paris cum semiviro comitatu.

With comic effect in the Georgics, I. 181: —

> tum variae illudant pestes: saepe exiguus mus.

To excuse the license of a spondee in the fifth foot, the poets used most frequently a word of four syllables, or sometimes a trisyllable; but in this latter case another word of at least three syllables ordinarily preceded this trisyllable: —

> armatumque auro circumspicit *Oriona*.
> perque hiemes aestusque et *inaequales autumnos*.

Vergil has twice (Æn. III. 12; VIII. 679) an ending borrowed from Ennius of this sort: —

> et magnis dis.

It is never the case in Latin that a spondaic verse has a dissyllable in the fifth or sixth place.

All these laws, with the exception of the use of five-syllabled words at the end of the verse, are equally valid for Greek poetry, although here exceptions are more numerous, especially as regards the verse-ending, and also the second foot where, on account of the frequency of the τομὴ κατὰ τρίτον τροχαῖον, dactylic words occur not rarely, and spondaic words much more rarely, as in the first verse of the Odyssey: —

ἄνδρα μοι ἔννεπε, Μοῦσα, πολύτροπον, ὃς μάλα πολλά.

A spondaic verse with a dissyllable in the fifth or sixth foot never occurs in Homer.

The rhythmical laws of the Pentameter are still more strict than those of the Hexameter.

In the Latin writers considered here, a dactylic or spondaic word never occurs in the second foot, and only once (Ovid, Pont. I. 6, 26) at the end of the verse do we find a monosyllabic enclitic word with preceding pyrrhic. Here, too, the Greeks are less strict than the Romans, but much stricter than in the Hexameter.

The Greeks and many Romans are wont to close the Pentameter with any polysyllable, but the most careful Romans (Tibullus, Propertius in Bks. IV. and V., and Ovid in most of his *post-exilian* poetry and always in his *pre-exilian*) close this verse with a dissyllable preceded by a word with trochaic ending — evidently in order in this way to make its termination like that of a Hexameter ending with a trisyllable.

26. Rhythmical Structure of the Remaining Metres.

The rhythmical laws of the Iambic Trimeter are precisely the same as those of the Hexameter. Consequently those verses cannot be approved which have at the Penthemimeral Cæsura a monosyllable with a preceding polysyllable, as in Horace:—

> diris *agam* vos, dira detestatio.

It is much worse when the third iambus closes with a word which has an iambic or spondaic (anapæstic) ending, as in the following examples:—

> regnante te *vides* ut imperium cadat.
> sed simplici *carmen* per omne evectus est.

For in these cases the verse is divided into two equal halves, and the Hephthemimeral Cæsura loses almost all its force. Such verses never occur in Horace and Phædrus, very seldom in the Greek tragedians, but more often in the Greek comedians.

Phædrus, in order not to dim the original iambic character of his verse, never places a word which itself has a spondaic or anapæstic ending at the end of the second, third, or fourth foot.

A monosyllable with preceding polysyllable at the end of a verse is bad, unless this monosyllable is enclitic, as in Sophocles:—

> οὐδ' ἂν δικαίως ἐς κακὸν πέσοιμί τι,

or in Phædrus:—

> timore mortis ille tum confessus est.

Horace avoids even this, but the Greek tragedians occasionally admit monosyllables at the end of the verse when they are not at all enclitic.

As regards systems and strophes in which Synapheia is allowed,—that is, in the Æolic, Doric, and dramatic,—it is clear that the rhythmical laws for cæsura and verse-endings must be less strictly observed at the time when the appreciation of the original metrical unity of the individual parts of system and strophe is still lively. Hence even Horace has sometimes a monosyllable with preceding polysyllable at the end of a logaœdic verse, as: —

> alme Sol, curru nitido *diem qui.*
> audivere, Lyce, di mea *vota, di.*

In the Alcaic hendecasyllabic an iambic word rarely occurs before the cæsura, as III. 1, 9 : —

> est ut *viro vir* latius ordinet.

In too close imitation of the Alcaic hendecasyllabic, Horace avoids similar words in the same places in the Alcaic enneasyllabic, except at I. 26, 11 in a proper name. In Horace, too, a spondaic word-ending never occurs as the second foot of the Sapphic hendecasyllabic, but, on the other hand, he has sometimes a dactylic word before the cæsural pauses of the Asclepiadean verses, as I. 6, 17 : —

> nos con*vivia*, nos | proelia virginum.

In general, wherever the strophes were only mechanically formed, or the verses written κατὰ στίχον, the rules were much more strictly observed, as is shown in the tragedies of Seneca.

SIXTH SECTION.

ENCLISIS AND TMESIS.

27. Enclisis.

IN order to correctly employ the rules already given, it is necessary to observe the rules of Enclisis and Tmesis. By Enclisis the enclitic word loses its own individuality and is merged into the preceding, so that *no* monosyllable really concludes the verse, as in the following example:—

ἀλλ' οὐδ' ὣς ἑτάρους ἐρρύσατο, ἱεμενός περ.
pectora quorum inter fluctus arrecta jubaeque.

It is natural that monosyllables which always stand in the second place, as μέν, δέ, γάρ, should be quite closely connected with the preceding word.

The cases of Enclisis in Greek are well known. In Latin, besides *que*, *ve*, *ne*, the monosyllabic forms of the indefinite pronoun *quis*, in combination with *si*, *ne*, *num*, *cum*, and in the formula *nesciöquis*, are used enclitically; also the pronouns *me*, *te*, *se*, *nos*, *vos* in combination with prepositions ending in *tra* and *ter*, as e.g. *inter*, *intra*. Finally the monosyllabic forms of the Indicative and Subjunctive of *sum* were sometimes used as enclitics, when a pyrrhic, tribrachic, or trochaic word preceded, but only on condition that the syllable before the auxiliary remained short.

It is to be noticed that *tum cum* usually becomes one word, as *satisesse, quopacto,* and often *priusquam, iamiam.*

28. Tmesis.

I. By Tmesis, in Homer and the tragedians, the preposition of a compound verb is frequently separated from its verb, generally by the interposition of one, or two or three short words, *e.g.*: —

ἐν δ' ἄρα οἱ φῦ χειρί, ἔπος τ' ἔφατ' ἔκ τ' ὀνόμαζε.

The preposition stands only rarely after the verb, evidently because it might then easily seem superfluous.

In Latin poetry, *cumque* is often separated from the relative pronouns and adverbs to which it belongs, and sometimes in prose. Thus in Horace: —

quem sors dierum *cumque* dabit.

Mihi cumque (Od. I. 32, 15) is a corrupt reading.

Note the passage in Vergil, Georg. III. 381, *septem subjecta trioni*, which was imitated by Ovid, Met. I. 64, *Scythiam septemque trionem*.

Elsewhere in the poets of the Augustan age, Tmesis occurs only in the case of prepositions which are also used independently as adverbs, as in Horace: —

circum
spectemus vacuam Romanis vatibus aedem.

Vergil, however, following the example of the older poets, has (Ecl. VIII. 17; Æn. IX. 288; X. 794) *prae*, and the negative *in* (always with a following *que*) thus separated; and Ovid imitates him in Met. XII. 497.

II. Another kind of Tmesis, not expressed in the text, occurs when the monosyllabic preposition or negative *in* of a compound word is for metrical reasons attracted to the preceding word.

This occurs on account of the cæsura in the following Horatian verses:—

>dum flagrantia *de* | torquet ad oscula,
>ut adsidens *in* | plumibus pullis avis,
>parentibusque *ab* | ominatus Hannibal;

and in this from Vergil:—

>magnanimi Iovis *in* | gratum adscendere cubile,

to release the first syllable from the second part of the compound. This kind of Tmesis occurs (very rarely) in Vergil in the Æneid, in Horace and Propertius, in Phædrus III. 15, 6; V. 7, 19, but not in Ovid and Tibullus.

SEVENTH SECTION.

ON THE TREATMENT OF SUCCESSIVE VOWEL SOUNDS.

29. Synizesis, Diæresis, Crasis, Elision, Hiatus.

INTRODUCTORY REMARKS. — When two vowels come together in the middle of a word or at the end of one word and beginning of another (in Latin also, when the first syllable or word ends with *m*, or the second syllable or word begins with *h*), there is a certain stopping of the voice, and a so-called *Hiatus* occurs. An attempt is made to avoid this in various ways, principally through a combination of the vowels by means of Contraction, Synizesis, and Elision. Among the Greeks those least sensitive to this Hiatus were the Ionians, as is shown by the Homeric poems. The Romans were on the whole much more sensitive in this matter than the Greeks.

Hiatus at the end of a word is the most unpleasant; less so in the middle of a compound, and still less so in a simple word. Hiatus in Homer is often only apparent, as the digamma frequently is to be considered as removing it; *e.g.* ϝεκηβόλος, ϝέπος, ϝοῖκος, ϝοῖνος, θεοϝείκελος, Ἀϝίδης, ἀϝέκων, Ἀτρεϝίδης. In course of time the Greeks and Romans became gradually less sensitive to hiatus, and therefore cases of harsh synizesis and elision became rare. However, greater freedom in the allowance of hiatus at the end of a word is not found in the most artistic poets, but in folk-poetry.

Hiatus appeared especially harsh when in the body of a word the first of the two vowels was long. This was quite frequent in Greek, but rare in Latin (*vocalis ante vocalem brevis*). Hence as early as Homer, the first vowel in οἶος, ἥρωος (Od. VI. 303) was sometimes shortened, and perhaps in δῆιος also. The Attic writers did the same in the case of ποιέω (for which in colloquial language ποέω was common), τοιοῦτος, etc., but generally only in the case of diphthongs whose second letter was ι. Thus for ειος, εια, ειον, occur frequently εος, ιος, in Latin ĕus, ĭus.

In Latin the first long vowel in combinations is regularly shortened; e.g. dĕhisco, prŏinde, prăeacutus.

In Latin of the Augustan age the penultimate vowel is long in the endings *ai, ei, ais, eis* from nominatives in *a, es, aius, -a, -um, eius, -a, -um,* as *aulai, Gai, dici, Mais, Circeis,* except *rĕi, spĕi, fidĕi;* the *i* is long in *fīo* and its derivatives except where followed by *ĕr* (Ovid: *omnia iam fient, fieri quae posse negabam*), and common (always long in Phædrus) in genitives in *ius* except *alīus* (contracted from *aliius*). The first vowel in *Diana* and *ohe* is also common.

Greek words when transferred to Latin retain their original quantity. For those ending in ειος, etc., see above. *Maeotis* Ov. Trist. III. 12, 2, is a corrupt reading.

Like vowels, especially when they have the same quantity, are usually contracted into one by the Attic writers.

In Latin of the Augustan age the combinations *aa, ee, oo,* are not found, except in the compound *coorior* (but *cŏperio*); somewhat oftener *ii, uu,* although until the time of Propertius, the genitive of substantives in *ius, ium* was always contracted, e.g. *fili, consili*. Hiatus was felt less when an *h* intervened, as *incoho, prehendo, nihil, mihi*, although even in these cases the contracted forms *prendo, nil*, and (rarely) *mi* occur; so always *vemens* for *vehemens*.

Compounds of *iacio*, in forms derived from the present, were written with one *i*, as *obicio*, although a weak *j* was sounded before the *i*. In *biiugus, quadriiugus*, ĭ only was sounded.

Until the time of Augustus *uo, vo* were written in place of *uu, vu*, not only at the beginning and in the middle of a word, but also at the end, e.g. *assiduos, servom*.

Other combinations of *u* and *o* with a vowel did not occur in Latin, except in compound and proper names, as *coalesco, Gai, Grais*, etc., while in Greek they were not uncommon. Of more frequent occurrence were *iu, ju, ui, vi*.

Ea, ei, eo, eu, ia, ie, io, ua, ue, uo are admissible, no matter whether the initial *i* and *u* are vowels or consonants. In Greek, on the contrary, simple *e* before a following vowel produced an unpleasant effect, as is shown by the frequent synizesis.

To avoid hiatus in the middle of a word, the Attic writers employ contraction very often, Homer much less frequently.

This contraction, however, is not rare in Latin, especially in many forms of perfects in *-vi*; usually in declension and conjugation; e.g. in the dative of the fourth declension *u* for *ui*, in the genitive and dative of the fifth *e* for *ei*, but also elsewhere: thus always *desse derrare*, usually *di, dis, idem, isdem* for *dei, deis, eidem, eisdem*.

30. Synizesis in Greek.

Synizesis hardly occurs in Greek except when the first vowel is ε, since this vowel, being the weakest, most easily combines with the following.

Synizesis is most acceptable in the arsis, *e.g.*: —

χρυσέῳ ἀνὰ σκήπτρῳ.
χρύσεον σκῆπτρον ἔχοντα.

But it often appears in the thesis: —

μῆνιν ἄειδε, θεά, Πηληϊάδεω 'Αχιλῆος.

Cases where the synizesis unites two short vowels to form the thesis, are also allowable, — as in Βέλεα, Πηλέος.

Homer and Archilochus employ synizesis especially in cases where contraction occurs in the later writers. The tragedians went still farther, following Pindar, not only in proper names, but also in other words; thus synizesis occurs in Πηλέᾶ, Θησέως, 'Ρέᾶ, Κρέων, frequently in Θεός and its cases, πόλεως, ἄστεως, ἐκπνέων, ἔᾶ, etc.

Synizesis appears especially in the thesis of the first and in the third foot of the Trimeter. As the Greeks did not know the consonantal ι, synizesis with iota seldom occurs. Thus in Homer we find Αἰγυπτίας, Ἱστίαιαν, also Ἐννυαλίῳ (but compare 34, beginning) and πότνα for πότνια, written out. This is rare and doubtful in the tragedians, particularly outside of the lyrical passages.

The cases of synizesis in 'Ερινύων (Eur. Iphig. Taur. 931, 970, 1456), δυοῖν (Soph. Oed. Rex, 640) rest on corrupt readings, and also in 'Ηλεκτρυώνη (Hes. Scut Herc. 16).

31. Synizesis in Latin.

I. As regards the Latin poets now under consideration, the first thing to be noticed is the change of *i* to *j* and (more rarely) *u* to *v*. This usually occurs in words which otherwise would not fit the metre. It never occurs in iambic and trochaic verse, and very seldom in logaoedic (Hor. Odes III. 4. 41; 6. 6, *consiljum*, *principjum*). It does not occur when two like consonants precede. Hence in Verg. Æn. VI. 653, we write *currum*. It is not allowed in the middle of compounds, and we must always read and write *semesus*, *semanimus*, *semhomo*, not *semiesus*, etc. To avoid this synizesis the poets often shortened the gen. plural "*ium*" to "*um*," e.g. *moderantum*, *sapientum;* sometimes they used in the fourth conjugation -*ibam* for -*iebam*, e.g. *lenibant*. The Greek words *Aiax*, *Graius*, *Maia*, *Troia*, had the consonantal *i* from earliest times. In other Greek words *i* and *u* did not become consonants, and hence we read: *ioat*, *iambus*, *Agaue*, *euangelium*, and always *Iulus;* for Hor. IV. 2, 2, is a corrupt reading.

This synizesis, which had already appeared in Ennius, occurs twenty-two times in Vergil, generally in words which would not otherwise fit into Hexameter verse, as in derivatives of *aries*, and *paries*, though sometimes in others, as *fluvjorum omnja*. *U* is changed to *v* only in *tenvis*, *tenvia*, *genva*. In Æn. I. 2, *Lavinaque* is to be read. Horace has in his hexameters *Nasidjeni*, *vindemjator*, *vjetis*, *Serviljo*, and *pitvita* twice. For his logaoedic verse, see above.

Synizesis occurs only twice in Ovid: Metam. VII. 151; XV. 718, *arjetis; Antjum*. XV. 709 does not belong in this category, as the antepenultimate in *promunturium* is short. In Propertius there are three cases of synizesis (in *abjegnae*, *abjegni*), but none in Tibullus.

Fortuitus and *conubium* never suffered synizesis, as *i* in the first word and *u* in the second were common. *Etiam* and *quoniam* have always vocalic *i*.

11. The second kind of Synizesis consists in the formation of a diphthong from two vowels. In the Augustan poets this occurs always (except in proper names) in dissyllabic or compound words. The diphthongs thus produced do not occur separately elsewhere in Latin. In prose of the best period *dein, deinde, deinceps, neuter, cui, huic*, have always the diphthong; on the other hand, the Romans pronounced *nūtiquam* and *antire*.

Dĕhinc, however, is generally dissyllabic, monosyllabic rarely in Vergil, and once only in Ovid and Propertius. In Hor. Sat. II. 3, 91 *quoad* is a monosyllable, and perhaps *prout* in II. 6, 67. *Reicere* is trisyllabic in Verg. Buc. 3, 96 (as *cuius* is monosyllabic in the Elegia ad Mersallam, 35), and *deicere* in Hor. Sat. I. 6, 39. Finally, the vocatives *Pompei* (Hor. Od. II. 7, 5) and *Vultei* (Ep. I. 7, 31) are dissyllabic, and *ei* is probably to be pronounced as *ÿ*.

Compounds of *circum* never suffer synizesis, but lose the *m*, e.g. *circuco, circuago*, or are divided by Tmesis, e.g. *circum errant*, Æn. II. 599.

In Greek words the diphthong ευ remains, as in *Harpyia;* also εν, e.g. *Orpheus*. Only in the Culex 117, 269, and in Phaedrus V. 1, 1 do we find *Orphĕus, Phalarĕus*. *Ei* in the genitive and (Eclog. 4, 57; Æn. V. 184) in the dative is diphthongal, and is so pronounced even in prose.

This synizesis (proper names excepted) is much more frequent in Plautus, who changes thereby words of three and more syllables when they are derived from dissyllables, as *suorum, puella, eamus, duellatores*.

III. The third kind of Synizesis, borrowed from the Greeks, occurs in the two last syllables of Greek proper names in εύς, the substantives *alveus* and *balteus*, and adjectives in *eus, ea, eum*, denoting material. It appears first in Catullus, and is employed only in dactylic metres, especially in the first and sixth foot of the Hexameter, and almost always in such a way that the last syllable is long. Vergil is fond of employing this form of synizesis as well as the others to express what is hard or dreadful, as Æn. VI. 280: —

    ferr*ei*que Eumenidum thalami et Discordia demens.

Vergil has it twenty-one times, in proper names and elsewhere; Ovid has it fourteen times; Horace, Sat. I. 8, 43; II. 2, 21, *cereā, ostreā;* Propertius, *Enipeo, Nereo, Prometheo;* Tibullus, *alveo*.

The genitive of words in εύς has been discussed above. In the Georgics, IV. 34, *alvearia* occurs with four syllables, where some write *alvaria*. Dissyllabic *Penei*, Georg. IV. 355, points to the nom. Πηνεός, as Ἀλφεός beside Ἀλφειός. Wherever adjectives have a shorter form this is employed to avoid synizesis, as *ahenus, eburnus, ilignus*.

32. Diæresis.

Diæresis is the division of a diphthong into two syllables. In most of the cases in Homer where diæresis was formerly assumed it is now plain that the older form of the word appears. Thus patronymics in -ειδης, like Πηλείδης, in which in Homer and Hesiod ε was always separated from ι, come from -εϝίδης; so ἔῃ from ἔσῃ, ἔϋ from ἔσυ, Λυκόοργος from Λυκόϝοργος, εἰδυῖα from ϝεϝιδυῖα. In Latin we find *siluae* with change of the *u*, in Hor. Od. I.

23, 4; Ep. 13, 2; in the Satires and in Phædrus *sŭetus*, *sŭesco;* in Ovid and Tibullus *sŏlŭo* and *vŏlŭo*, but only in compounds; in Propertius *Vĕius*.

33. Elision.

GENERAL REMARKS.—The meeting of two vowels at the end and beginning of two words appeared to the classic poets much less admissible than hiatus in the middle of the word. Latin words ending in *m* were considered as ending in a vowel, and those beginning with *h* were regarded as vocalic also.

Hiatus was considered especially harsh in the case of short final syllables or those ending in *m*, as these were spoken more rapidly than the long. Among the short finals, ε and ο in Greek, and ĕ and ĭ in Latin, had a particularly weak sound.

The meeting of two like vowels was especially disagreeable.

To avoid hiatus, Elision of the final vowel was employed. This is a false name, for the final vowel except in *que, ve, ne,* and the monosyllabic particles in ε, as τέ, γέ, δέ, was never completely dropped, but when a long syllable followed or was demanded by the metre, the final was combined with the succeeding vowel into a kind of diphthong. If the following vowel was short, the final was so weakened by rapid utterance, that it was not considered from a metrical point of view. This last kind of elision was regarded as the harsher. In Greek, the later writers usually drop those final vowels which are not counted metrically, and mark their omission by the apostrophe, *e.g.* οὐλομένην, ἢ μύρι᾽ Ἀχαιοῖς. This is faulty in so far as it makes no distinction between the two different kinds of elision just described.

Elision in Greek.

In the discussion of Elision and Hiatus, Greek and Latin usages must be sharply distinguished.

34. Elision in Greek. Crasis. Aphæresis.

In Greek the combination of a long vowel or one that is not otherwise elided, with a following long vowel, is of comparatively rare occurrence, but when it does occur it is usually when the words καί, δή, μή, ὦ, ἦ, ἤ, ἐγώ, μοί, σοί, τοί, πρό, ὅ, ἅ, come first, or ἄρα, ἄν, οὐ, follow, as *e.g.* in Homer at the beginning of the verse:—

ἦ οὐκ ἀίεις.

In Homer, also, the following cases are to be noted:—

Od. I. 226,	εἰλαπίνη ἠὲ γάμος;
Il. XVIII. 458,	υἱεῖ ἐμῷ ὠκυμόρῳ;
perhaps, too, II. 651,	Ἐνυαλίῳ ἀνδρεϊφόντῃ;
and I. 277,	μήτε σύ, Πηλείδη, ἔθελ'.

This union of two vowels was expressed, frequently by the Attic writers, rarely by Homer, in the writing itself by means of Crasis, principally when the article or one of the short words ὦ, ὅ, ἅ, καί, πρό, μοί, σοί, τοί, came first, as *e.g.* οὕνεκα, τἀνδρί, τἄλλα, etc. It can also be counted a case of crasis when ε or (seldom) α at the beginning of a word is elided (aphæresis) if a long vowel precedes, *e.g.* ἐξελῶ 'κ τῆς οἰκίας. This happens principally with the augment, single prepositions, adverbs, conjunctions, or other very common words, like ἐγώ, ἐστίν, ἔστω, ἔσται, as well as ἀνά and ἀπό, especially in the Attic poets, who employ crasis and aphæresis usually in dialogue.

ἄ, ε, ο, are cut out of the verse without hesitation, although the optative ending ειε, the imperative ἴδε, and the genitive οιο, are not thus elided. Further, ι was elided in the verb-endings σι, μι, θι, τι; in Homer the ι of the dative plural, and rarely that of the singular, as (Il. V. 5; X. 277):—

ἀστέρ' ὀπωρινῷ ἐναλίγκιος,

χαῖρε δὲ τῷ ὄρνιθ' Ὀδυσσεύς.

In the same way θι in ὅθι, ἄλλοθι, αὐτόθι, τηλόθι. It is doubtful whether ὅτι is elided in Homer, for in such cases Bekker writes ὅτε. Short υ is never elided.

Again αι (which very early appears to have suffered a weakening of the diphthongal sound in many forms, and sounded to the Greeks of the latest period always as short ε) was elided in the forms of the Passive and Infinitive, as βούλομαι, δοῦναι. Once αι in the nominative plural is elided, Il. XI. 272, ὀξεῖ' ὀδύναι. The elision of οι in μοί, σοί, τοί, as Il. I. 170, οὐδέ σ' ὀίω; VI. 165, ὅς μ' ἔθελεν, is very rare and questionable.

35. Elision in Latin.

Compare first the general remarks on Elision, **33**. The means which the Romans employed to avoid hiatus were exactly the same as those of the Greeks. The harsher character of the Latin language was shown by this fact, that in general no account was taken in the metre of a final vowel occurring in the hiatus, whether long or short. Compare for Elision in Latin, Cic. Orator, 44, 150; 45, 152; Quint. IX. 4, 33.

As would be expected, the harshest form of elision was that of long vowels, particularly of the diphthong *ae*; less harsh was the elision of syllables ending in *m*, which were pronounced short, but in which the closing consonant still kept some sound; easiest of all was the elision of short syllables. Elision was harsher in the cases where the second vowel was short than where it was long, as has been already remarked.

In the Æneid I. 1–80 there are twenty-one cases of the elision of short vowels (among them fourteen cases of *que*, *ne*), twelve cases of the elision of syllables ending in *m*, and eight of long vowels, one of the diphthong *ae*.

The elision of a vowel preceded by a vowel without a consonant (*vocalis pura*) seldom occurs if the first vowel is long, as Æn. X. 179, *Alpheae ab origine*.

The best poets seldom elide Greek endings, as in *Ino*, *Penelope* (Ovid never).

As regards the compass of the word, elision seems most harsh in monosyllables which are long or end in *m*, and these were never elided if they belonged to a regular declension or conjugation, except *qui* (nom. sing.), *me*, *te*, *de*, *tu*, *mi* (*mihi*), *sum*.

Further, since by the laws of Latin accent, the final vowel was less emphatically pronounced in words with spondaic, trochaic, or tribrachic endings, than in those with cretic, dactylic, iambic, and pyrrhic endings, the former class of words suffer elision more frequently.

Again, elision is considered harsher when the second syllable has the acute or circumflex accent, than when it has the grave or none at all.

Monosyllabic pronouns (except the interrogative *quis*, *qui*), prepositions, conjunctions, *atque* when the *e* is elided, and the most common monosyllabic adverbs, like *hic*, *ut*, *haud*, have the grave accent.

From what has been said, it is not surprising that the best poets never elide iambic words before acute, circumflex, or short syllables (except twice in Phædrus, III. 7, 15;

V. 9, 4, *veni ergo; tace inquit*), and cretic words almost never. Of the poets considered here, Horace alone in the Satires allows the elision of cretic words before following short syllables.

Dactylic or pyrrhic words ending in *m*, *a*, *o*, are treated in the same way, though somewhat less strictly.

In the oldest Roman poets, Plautus, Terence, and sometimes in Lucilius, there are many, and often harsh cases of elision, remarkably few in the Annals of Ennius; in Vergil a considerable number, but rarely of a harsh character. In the Satires Horace has more and harsher cases of elision than in the Epistles; still fewer in the Odes and Epodes. In Propertius the cases of elision are more numerous and harsher than in Tibullus. The most polished of the poets in this respect was Ovid, and the later writers for the most part followed his example. To illustrate this, in the first book of the Metamorphoses, which as epic poetry contains an especially large number of cases of elision, long syllables are elided only 8 times; syllables ending in *m*, 23 times; short syllables, 129 times. On the other hand, the corresponding numbers in the first book of the Æneid are 85, 97, 173.

In general, elision is most frequent in the epic hexameter, and less frequent in the didactic, bucolic, and elegiac pentameter, and in the logaœdic and iambic verse of Horace.

Vergil frequently employs numerous or harsh elisions in the painting of difficult or fearful situations (Æn. III. 658; IX. 427) : —

monstr*um* horrend*um* inform*e* ingens.
non *me!* adsum qui fec*i*; in me convertite ferrum.

Those cases do not properly belong to elision where *est* (sometimes also *es*) stands after a vowel or *m*. In this case *est* (*es*) loses its vowel, and we read *magnumst*, *illast*, *ille's*.

36. Differences in Elision in Greek and Latin Verse.

For Greeks and Romans alike this rule holds good, that elision very seldom occurs before the first or after the last, or the next to the last syllable of the verse.

Elision after the last syllable occurs properly only in verses which are united by Synaphcia, as in anapæstic systems.

In such verses in Greek elision is tolerably frequent, and even a few times in the Odes of Horace (in Horace the preceding syllable is always long, and the elision never occurs at the end of the strophe).

The Alexandrian poets, and imitating them the Romans, falsely explaining some Homeric verses, occasionally (very seldom except in Vergil) allow elision at the end of a hexameter. The Romans do this only when another hexameter follows. Such exceptional verses are wrongly called hypermetrical (*versus hypermetri*). The preceding syllable is always long.

With the exception of two verses in Vergil ending in *m*, *e* is the only vowel thus elided, especially in *que*. Vergil sometimes employs such a verse-ending in rhythmical painting, as Æn. VI. 602, 3 (cf. also IV. 629, 30):—

> quos super atra silex iam iam lapsura cadenti*que*
> imminet adsimilis.

In Sophocles, but not in Æschylus and Euripides, elision sometimes occurs at the end of the trimeter, generally if δέ or τε stands at the end; always with a preceding long syllable, e.g. Oed. Rex 29 ff. : —

ὑφ' οὗ κενοῦται δῶμα Καδμεῖον, μέλας δ'
Ἅιδης στεναγμοῖς καὶ γόοις πλουτίζεται.

Elision before the last syllable of the verse occurs in Horace's Satires and Epistles, as well as in the Odes the verses of which can be united by Synaphcia, but not at the end of the strophe.

Of the other poets considered here Vergil alone twice elides *atque* after the sixth thesis (Æn. IX. 57; 440).

The Greeks not infrequently placed monosyllables with a following οὐ at the beginning of the verse, as Od. I. 298: —

ἦ οὐκ ἀίεις;

Elision occurs at the beginning of a hexameter several times in the Satires of Horace, once (3, 48) in the Eclogues of Vergil, but never in the other poets. Of course no account is made here of those cases where a so-called hypermetric verse precedes.

On the other hand, elision is never prevented by a following or preceding caesura or by punctuation or even by a change of the persons speaking, e.g. (Æn. I. 96; Il. I. 2; Hippol. 612; Æn. III. 98; Soph. El. 1502) : —

contigit oppetere! o Danaum fortissime gentis!

οὐλομένην, ἣ μυρί' Ἀχαιοῖς ἄλγε' ἔθηκεν.

ἡ γλῶσσ' ὀμώμοκ' : ἀλλ' ὁ νοῦς ἀνώματος.

et nati nat*orum* et qui nascentur ab illis.

βάλλ' αἰεὶ δὲ πυραὶ νεκύων καίοντο θαμειαί.

Orest. ἀλλ' ἔρφ'. Ægisth. ὑφηγοῦ. Or. σοὶ βαδιστέον πάρος.

The better poets, however, like Tibullus and Ovid, avoid eliding, in general, a long syllable in the third arsis or where there is a decided stop. They also elide very rarely a long syllable at the cæsura.

The greatest freedom and frequency of elision in the Latin Hexameter is noticed in the arsis of the first, the thesis of the second, and also in the whole of the fourth foot, except when the Hephthemimeral Cæsura occurs. In the other places elision is far less frequent, especially in the arsis of the second and the thesis of the sixth.

In the Pentameter the elision of syllables which are either long or end in *m*, is in the best poets mostly restricted to the first arsis or the second thesis. Elision at the cæsural pause does not occur in Propertius, Tibullus, and Ovid; never after the cæsura in Ovid, and almost never in Propertius and Tibullus. In the second half of the Pentameter Ovid never elides long syllables or those ending in *m*. Horace allows elision not infrequently before and after the cæsura of the lyric measures, except in the Sapphic Hendecasyllabic, where it almost never occurs.

37. Hiatus.

GENERAL REMARKS.—When a vowel at the end of a word remains unchanged before a following vowel, Hiatus is occasioned. The harshest case of this is when vowels having the same sound come together, as Od. XI. 596, λᾶαν ἄνω ὤθεσκε. On the other hand, hiatus is most allowable where the elision of the final syllable would be harsh.

38. Hiatus in Greek.

When a long final syllable occurs in the thesis of a dactylic measure, hiatus with the following vowel is allowed, *e.g.*: —

μῆνιν ἄειδε θεά, Πηληιάδεω Ἀχιλῆος.

So, too, in the arsis when the long vowel is shortened: —

ἄνδρα μοι ἔννεπε, Μοῦσα, πολύτροπον.

Hiatus also occurs with short vowels, especially such as are seldom or never elided, as with υ and ι in the dative singular, in the genitive οιο, in τί, περί, ὅ, ἀνά = ἀνάστηθι.

It is very rare in the thesis, and only admissible in the regular Penthemimeral and Hephthemimeral Caesura, as Il. II. 781; V. 576; VIII. 556; XXIV. 285.

An unpleasant effect is produced if the long vowel of the arsis remains long, as sometimes is the case in the first and fourth foot of the hexameter, and especially with monosyllables, as *e.g.*: —

κούρη Ἰκαρίοιο, περίφρων Πηνελόπεια.

χλαῖνάν τ' ἠδὲ χιτῶνα τά τ' αἰδῶ ἀμφικαλύπτει.

ἢ χιόνι ψυχρῷ ἢ ἐξ ὕδατος κρυστάλλῳ.

Hiatus of short syllables is most harsh in the case of a final ε in monosyllabic and trochaic words, and least harsh in dactylic words. In these last, hiatus occurs most frequently in the first and fourth foot (bucolic caesura). Again, hiatus is sometimes allowed on account of the τομὴ κατὰ τρίτον τροχαῖον, as *e.g.*: —

ἀλλ' ἀκέουσα κάθησο. ἐμῷ δ' ἐπιπείθεο μύθῳ.

Punctuation also relieves the harshness of hiatus in a similar way. Of course those cases in Homer where the

Hiatus in Greek. 105

following word has the digamma, or in earliest times began with a consonant, have nothing to do with hiatus, as *e.g.*: —

στέμματ' ἔχων ἐν χερσὶ Ϝεκηβόλου Ἀπόλλωνος.

So *e.g.* ἅλις = *satis*, ἕδος = *sedes*, ἕξ = *sex*, ἕπομαι = *sequor*, ὅς = *suus*. Cf. *e.g.* O.l. XVII. 303 : δυνήσατο οἷο ἄνακτος.

Cases of hiatus in Homer and Hesiod, which are not comprehended under the rules already mentioned, rest either on a corrupt text or are to be explained by old forms of the words now unknown, but which removed the supposed hiatus.

Homer was the model of the later epic poets, who through misunderstanding introduced hiatus in places where in Homer's time none existed because of the digamma. But hiatus occurred in this epic poetry less frequently than in Homer, and still less often in the bucolic and didactic poets.

In the fifth century after Christ Nonnus and his imitators restricted hiatus to a few cases with long final syllable.

Hiatus occurs more rarely in the elegiac hexameter, and still more so in the pentameter, where it appears usually in the first foot and the first dactyl after the caesura. At the caesura it is doubtful.

Cases of the hiatus of long syllables with shortening in the arsis of anapaestic metres are not uncommon.

In the iambic trimeter and trochaic tetrameter of tragedy hiatus very seldom occurs in the thesis, and then before a stop, or where the same word is repeated, as Æsch. Agam. 1216: —

ὀτοτοῖ, Λύκει' Ἄπολλον. οἳ ἐγώ, ἐγώ.

Such examples stand mostly by themselves, outside of the verse. Hiatus is not allowed in the arsis.

39. Hiatus in Latin.

Compare the general remarks in 37.

Hiatus occurs extremely seldom in the Roman dactylic poets, especially in the arsis of the foot. In Vergil, the hiatus of a short final syllable occurs only twice. Ecl. II. 53; Æn. I. 405 : —

> addam cerea pru*nă*. honos erit huic quoque pomo.
> et vera incessu patuit de*ă*. ille ubi matrem, —

in each case before a decided stop.

Long monosyllabic words or those ending in *m* allow hiatus in the arsis if a short syllable follows; as once in the Satires of Horace : —

> si me amas inquit; cocto num adest honor idem?

This kind of hiatus is very common in Plautus and Terence, but generally in cases where these small words form the first syllables of resolved iambic or trochaic theses. The first kind of hiatus occurs sometimes in Vergil, *e.g.* Æn. VI. 507 : —

> tĕ, amice, nequivi.

Elsewhere iambic or cretic words are sometimes shortened in the arsis (as Ennius had already done), *e.g.* in Vergil (Ecl. 3, 79; Æn. III. 211) : —

> et longum formose vale valĕ inquit Iolla.
> insulă Ionio in magno.

This hiatus occurs sometimes in Vergil; in Propertius once, IV. 11, 17; in Ovid three times, Am. II. 13, 21; Met. I. 155; III. 501; the conjectural reading in Horace Ep. II. 3, 65, *diŭ aptaque remis*, is incorrect.

Spondaic words at the hiatus occur only in Horace Ep. 5. 100 (probably a corrupt reading) and Vergil, Georg. I. 437 : —

et Esquilin*ae* alites.

Glauc*ō* et Panope*ae* et Inoo Melicertae.

In this verse in imitation of Euphorion, the spondaic word of the first foot is preserved unshortened with the hiatus.

In the poets considered here hiatus in the arsis, except in Hor. Ep. 5, 100, and hiatus in the thesis, except in the dactylic tetrameter *ossibus et capiti inhumato*, Hor. Odes I. 28, occur only in hexameter verse. The final syllable is always long, except in three cases, Tibullus I. 5, 33; Prop. III. 15, 1; 32, 45, where the syllable ends in *m*; and this syllable is always the final of a polysyllabic word except in Verg. Æn. IV. 235:—

quid struit aut qua spe inimica in gente moratur.

Most poets allow hiatus only in the regular caesuras of the hexameter or before Greek words, *e.g.*:—

Nereidum matr*i* et Neptu*no* Aegaeo.

Vergil, however, in imitation of Ennius, sometimes allows hiatus at other points in the verse, at the end of words having an anapaestic ending or before a stop:—

evolat infelix et femineo ululatu.

si pereo, hominum manibus periisse juvabit.

He allows this hiatus in the thesis perhaps forty times; Ovid has it only twenty-six times; Horace once (Ep. 13, 3) besides the example quoted above.

Finally, it is to be noticed that the interjections *o* and *a*, both in thesis and arsis, before long and short vowels, can be kept long by the poets, *e.g.*:—

o et de Latio, o et de gente Sabina; o ego laevus;

but not *heu*, which never occurs in a hiatus (*eheu* is always to be read instead of *heu heu*).

EIGHTH SECTION.

LENGTHENING BY POSITION.

40. General Remarks.

A SHORT vowel followed by two or more consonants or by ζ, ξ, ψ, was usually considered long, although in most cases it was pronounced as short.

A short vowel was always regarded as long, when it was followed in the *same* word by two or more consonants, except a mute and a liquid; *e.g.* τέμνω, Εὐρυσθεύς, ἐκλέγω, *omnis*, *aspicio*, *adluo*.

41. Greek.

Generally in Homer a short vowel is lengthened before a mute and a liquid, whether these occur in the same word or at the beginning of the following. Only if the second vowel is λ or ρ (except βλ, γλ, δλ), a final vowel sometimes, and a medial vowel less often, remains short.

Hence the reading in Il. XVI. 857, λιποῦσ' ἀνδροτῆτα καὶ ἥβην, is wholly corrupt and long since rejected.

Homer's example was followed by the older epic poets, and the iambic writers like Archilochus.

On the other hand, in the Old Comedy, only βλ, γλ usually, and γμ, γν, δμ, δν always, lengthen a preceding short vowel (*correptio Attica*). The tragedians conform more to the example of Homer.

Consonants, not mutes and liquids, always render the preceding vowel long, although Homer shortens final syllables preceding the words σκέπαρνον, Σκάμανδρος, Ζάκυνθος, Ζέλεια, as otherwise these would not fit the metre.

42. Latin.

Plautus and Terence did not recognize the lengthening of a preceding short vowel by a following mute and liquid except *gm* and *gn*, and usually in other cases, especially in dissyllables, *e.g. ĭlle, ĭste, ĭmmo, ĕsse, fĕrĕntarius*, disregarded the rules of position.

On the other hand, the dactylic poets followed the Greek system in the middle of a word at least, although a mute and liquid exercised a lengthening force on the preceding short less frequently than in Homer. Hence many combinations of consonants, which appear frequently in Greek, are quite foreign to the Latin language.

Cycnus is always written with a short *y*; in *lātrare* the *a* is long by nature.

A final short vowel remains short when followed by a mute and liquid except *gn*.

Hence after a preceding short final vowel we must write *Cnosus, Cnidus, narus, natus, narus*, instead of *Gnosus*, etc.

Short final syllables before other combinations of consonants appear usually only in those cases where *syllaba anceps* is allowed, as in Horace, Ep. 17, 26:—

> levare tenta spiritu praecordia.

The oldest Roman poets sometimes permit a short vowel to retain its quantity before impure *s* (*s* followed by a consonant), especially after a dactyl in the first and fifth foot of the hexameter. This usage is limited in the Augustan poets to the words *Zacynthus, Scamander, smaragdus* (*zmaragdus*), with these few exceptions; in the Satires of Horace; Propertius; Vergil, Æn. XI. 309; Ovid, Halieutica, 120; Phædrus, III. 3, 14; app. 9, 12.

Lengthening of a short final syllable when the next word begins with two or three consonants, does not occur in the poets considered here, except in Tibullus I. 5, 18; 6, 34; and in general it is very rare.

NINTH SECTION.

HOMERIC PROSODY.

43. Peculiarities of Prosody in Homer.

In consequence of the mobility of the Ionic dialect, in Homer's time the quantity of many syllables might vary, or at least the lengthening of short syllables would be less offensive to the ear, especially in words which otherwise would fit the hexameter metre either with difficulty or not at all, and in words of very frequent occurrence. The vowels, α, ι, υ, show the most frequent exceptions to the usual quantity.

Thus the penult is common in Homer in the names of the chief heroes of the poem, Ἀχιλεύς and Ὀδυσεύς; the first syllable is often lengthened in ἀνήρ, Ἄρης, Ἀπόλλωνος, etc., ἀτάλλω, ἵλαος, πρίν, πιαίνω, τίω, ῥύομαι, ὕδωρ, ἴω; always lengthened in ἀθάνατος, ἀκάματος, ἀπονέοντο, ἀγοράασθε, διογενές, Ζεφυρίη, πιόμενος, Πριαμίδης, δυναμένοιο, θυγατέρεσσι. Sometimes this lengthening is expressed in the script, as in ἠνεμόεις instead of ἀνεμόεις, ἠΰς instead of ἐΰς, Διώνυσος instead of Διόνυσος. The liquids λ, μ, ν, ρ, also ς and occasionally π and δ, helped on the lengthening of short vowels, because they were easily doubled in pronunciation, especially in compounds and after the augment. Thus for instance καταλοφάδεια. This lengthening is frequently expressed by the doubling of the consonant; thus in ἔλλαβε, ἔμμαθε, ἐτάνυσσε, ὅππως, and also in Ἀχιλλεύς and Ὀδυσσεύς. For μέλανι (Il. XXIV. 79) another reading gives μείλανι.

For well-known reasons, metrical licenses not permitted elsewhere occur frequently in the first foot; thus *e.g.* διά (Il. III. 357); often ἐπειδή as a Molossus (– – –). Many cases of lengthening of short syllables are explained by an older form, as in the first syllable of ἴ(ϝ)ῐες, and the second in ἀπο(ϝ)ειπών. Thus the forms βαθύρ.οος, ἔννεπε, σύνεχές, ἔδδεισεν, came from βαθύσροος, ἔνσεπε, σύνσεχές, ἔδ(ϝ)εισεν. In the same way ἔσσευᾳ, φιλομμειδής point to an original ἔσ(ϝ)εα, φιλοσμειδής. The long vowel in ὄφις (Il. XII. 208) allows the conjecture of an old form ὄπφις. The digamma has remained as a vowel in εὔαδον and αὐτάρ.

The later hexameter poets adopted a large number of the Homeric lengthenings already described, partly without knowing the reason for their existence. In some cases the usual Homeric quantity remained the regular one in almost all later poets, as *e.g.* in ἀθάνατος, ἀκάματος.

In Homer the first syllable of καλός and ἴσος is always long, but in the Attic poets short.

In the arsis of the foot a short syllable is sometimes lengthened, especially the vowel ι, *e.g.* in ἱστίη, ὀπωρινῷ, ὑπεροπλίῃσι, etc. On the other hand, instead of ἧνιν and βλοσυρῶπις we have the other readings ἧνιν and βλοσυρώπις with long finals.

The long vowel in the arsis of these two verse-beginnings πολλὰ λισσομένη and πολλὰ ῥυστάζεσκεν has not yet been sufficiently explained; in πυκνὰ ῥωγαλέην it is necessitated by the older form ϝρωγαλέος.

The shortening of long syllables, on the other hand, is a very doubtful matter. In φοινικύεσσα the ι is not shortened, but οε united by synizesis. The shortening of η and ω in the Subjunctive, *e.g.* βούλεται, εἴδομεν, ἴομεν, is by no means an arbitrary process, but based upon older formations.

In general, many old forms remained in the language of Homer, which were employed along with those later forms which were the more usual at the time when the Iliad and Odyssey were composed. This fact explains on the one hand the astonishing fulness and variety of Homeric forms, and on the other their uncertainty and irregularity.

TENTH SECTION.

LATIN PROSODY.

44. Peculiarities of Latin Prosody.

In the Roman poets any variation in the quantity of the stem syllable is very rare, except in some proper names. It is to be noticed, however, that in dactylic and logaœdic metres the first syllable is long in *religio, religiosus, reliquiae* (on account of the old form *red* in these words, originally written *rell*); in the perfects *reperi, repuli, retudi, retuli,* and also elsewhere (*rēcido*) the first syllable always remained long. In iambic metres we find only *rĕligio, rĕligiosus, rĕliquiae*.

On the other hand, the Latin language, in a manner corresponding to its barytone character, allowed frequent shortening of final syllables.

While, for example, in Plautus not a few endings which afterwards were shortened, of nouns and verbs in *r*, *s*, *t*, which had a long vowel in the genitive and in the second person, still appear as long, after Ennius in dactylic poetry these are regularly shortened. The long syllable remained only in *iīt* and *petīt* (to compensate for the dropped *v*), sometimes in *sanguis* and *pulvis*, and often in the 2d Pers. Sing. of the Perf. and Fut. Perf. Subj. Thus for example Hor. (IV. 7, 20) : —

quae dederīs animo.

Peculiarities of Latin Prosody. 115

The first syllable of -*imus*, -*itis*, of these tenses is common. Greek endings retain their original quantity. Even words ending in *ā* sometimes keep this quantity, e.g. *Andromedā*, *Electrā*.

Further, it was customary from an early date to shorten a number of iambic words which were especially common. Plautus and Terence carry this very far, but in the best dactylic poets it is principally the following words which appear shortened: *ego*, *duo*, *here*, *bene*, *male*, *cito*, *modo*, *ita*, *quia*, *nisi*, *quasi*. The final is common in *mihi*, *tibi*, *sibi*, *ibi*, *ubi*. *Ubinam* and *ubivis* have a short vowel; *ubīque*, *utrŏbīque*, *ibīdem*, a long vowel. *I* is long in *utī*, *sicutī*, *velutī*, but short in *utĭnam*, *utĭque*, *nutĭquam*.

The poets went still farther with the ending *o*; for while the older dactylic poets shortened the *o* only in some iambic substantives and verbs, as *homo*, *puto*, *dabo*, and always in *nesciŏ quis;* in Vergil, Horace, Tibullus, and Propertius, some cretic feet are also shortened, as *Poliŏ*, *dixerŏ;* in Horace's Satires *quomodŏ;* in Propertius *findŏ*.

Ovid, except in the Metamorphoses, shortens variously cretic and also spondaic words (always *Sulmŏ*, *Nasŏ*), among them the adverb *ergŏ*. Of the poets of the first century after Christ many shorten the *o* generally in substantives (except in Greek words like *Dīdō*), in verbs, in several adverbs, and the numerals *ambŏ*, *octŏ*, and finally (though very rarely) in the ablative of the Gerund. The *o* of the interjection *io* is always long.

ELEVENTH SECTION.

LENGTHENING.

45. Lengthening by the Thesis at the End of a Word.

GENERAL REMARKS. — A short syllable at the end of a word could be lengthened more easily than one in the middle of the word, since in the former case a short pause of the voice naturally ensues.

46. Greek.

Hence in Homer, the lengthening of short vowels occurs especially before those liquids λ, μ, ν, ρ, which are easily doubled, and occasionally, too, before δ and σ, though in connection with this it must be noticed that words now beginning with the former letters then began quite frequently with two consonants; e.g. ϝρήγνυμι, σμοῖρα, σνευρή, δϝέος.

The letter ρ often has the effect of lengthening a preceding short vowel in the dialogue as well as in the lyric parts of the Attic drama.

A final syllable ending in a consonant is also unhesitatingly lengthened. This happens generally in the caesura or before punctuation, but rarely in the first or sixth thesis.

Cases where the following word has the digamma, as Il. I. 74, μέλποντες ϝεκάϝεργον, are of course not counted here.

The later epic poets before Nonnus imitate Homer with more or less frequency; less often still the didactic and bucolic poets, sometimes without understanding the linguistic reasons for their licenses.

In lyric and dramatic measures the lengthening of final syllables is not produced by the simple force of the thesis, especially in the iambic and trochaic verses. In the dactylic pentameter, also, such lengthening is very rare and usually doubtful, even in the first half of the verse, and at the caesura itself.

47. Latin.

In this respect also the Romans followed much stricter rules than the Greeks.

Monosyllables are never lengthened, nor short syllables ending in a vowel, except that Vergil (Æn. III. 464) seems to have permitted *gravia*. In the same way (Ennius Ann. 149), *aquila*. The enclitic *que* is sometimes lengthened in Vergil, in imitation of Homer, and after him in Ovid's Metamorphoses, but always when preceded by a dactylic or spondaic word, and followed by a second *que* with the foot _ _ ∪ or ∪ ∪ _ ∪, e.g. (Æn. III. 91):—

> limaquē laurusque dei totusque moveri.

This is allowed only when two consonants or a double consonant, a liquid or *s*, follow. Elsewhere Vergil, in imitation of Ennius, lengthens a final syllable (as in a case of hiatus) not only at the caesura and before Greek words, but also when three short syllables close a word or punctuation follows it. Thus we find not only (Ecl. X. 69; Georg. I. 138):—

> omnia vincit a*mor*. et nos cedamus amori.
> Pleia*das* Hyadas claramque Lycaonis Arcton.

But also (Georg. II. 5; Æn. XI. 111):—

> muneri*b*us, tibi pampineo gravi*dus* autumno.
> ora*tis?* equidem et vivis concedere vellem.

There are about fifty cases in Vergil of the lengthening of final syllables ending in a consonant.

The other poets allow this lengthening only at the regular cæsura, or before following Greek words, and all very rarely. Ovid ten times; Horace (in the logacedic measures also) eleven times: Sat. I. 4, 82; 5, 90; II. 1, 82; 2, 47; 3, 1; 260; Odes I. 3, 36; 13, 6; II. 6, 14; III. 16, 26; 24, 5; Tibullus four times; Propertius three times.

This lengthening does not occur in iambic and trochaic measures.

INDEX.

A.

Accius, 25, 26.
Adonius, 55.
Æschylus, 20.
Alcæus, 17.
Alcaic Decasyllabic, 66.
Alcaic Hendecasyllabic, 66.
Alcaic Strophe, 68.
Alcman, 19.
Alexandrians, 23, 24.
Alfius Avitus, 34.
Alliteration, 46.
Anacreon, 18.
Anacreontic, 18.
Anacrusis, 40.
Ananius, 18.
Anapæstic Metres, 55, 56.
Antiquarian tendency in Roman Versification, 33.
Antistrophe, 19, 43.
Aphæresis, 97.
Archilochian Strophe, 70, 71.
Archilochian Systems, 72.
Archilochus, 17.
Arion, 19.
Aristophanes, 21.
Aristophanic, *see* Lesser Sapphic, 66.
Arsis, 38.
    Resolution of, 48, 49.
Asclepiadean Strophes, 69, 70.
Asynartete, 41.
Ausonius, 35, 66, 67.
Avienus, 34.

B.

Bacchylides, 19.
Basis, 38, 40.
Besantinus, 24.

C.

Cæsura, 5.
Cæsuras of the Hexameter, 51–54.
Cæsuras of the Trimeter, 59, 60.
Callinus, 16.
Calvus, 28.
Cantica, 26.
Catalectic Verse, 41.
Catullus, 28, 29.
Chæremon, 23.
Choral Lyric, 18, 19.
Claudianus, 32.
Crasis, 97.

D.

Dactylic Metres, 50–55.
Dancing, 24.
Development of Ancient Versification, 13, 14.
Diæresis, 32.
Dialogue in Attic Drama, 20, 21.
Dialogue in Roman Drama, 25, 26.
Dipody, 40.
Distich, 16, 54, 67.
Dithyramb, 19.
Dochmiac Rhythm in Attic Drama, 22.

Dosiadas, 24.
Drama, Attic, 20–23.
Drama, Roman, 25–27.

E.
Elegiambic Verse, 67.
Elision, 96, 97.
   in Greek, 97, 98.
   in Latin, 98–101.
   variation in, 101–103.
Enclisis, 86.
Ennius, 25–28.
Epode, 43.
   of Horace, 71–73.
   in Doric Lyric, 19.
   in Attic Drama, 21.
Euphony, 40, 41, 44.
Euripides, 21.

F.
Fronto, 33.

G.
Georgius Pisides, 34, 35.
Glyconic Verse, 64.
Greater Archilochian, 66.
Greater Asclepiadean, 65.
Greater Sapphic, 65.
Gregorius Nazianzenus, 34.

H.
Hesiod, 15.
Hexameter, 50–55.
Hiatus, 103.
   in Greek, 104, 105.
   in Latin, 106, 107.
Hipponactean Iambics and Trochees, 18, 29.
Hipponactean Strophe, 71.
Hipponax, 17, 18.
Homer, 15, 16.
Horace, 30, 31.
Hymns, Christian, 34, 35.
Hypercatalectic Verse, 41.
Hypermeter, 101.

I.
Iambelegiac Verse, 67.
Iambic Metres, 57, 62.
Iambic System, 72.
Ibycus, 19.
Ictus, 42.
Ionic Decameter, 64.
Ionic Strophe, 71.
Ithyphallic Verse, 63.

L.
Lævius, 28.
Lesser Asclepiadean, 65.
Lesser Sapphic, 66.
Logaœdic Metres, 41, 64–66.
Lucilius, 26–28.
Lucretius, 28, 29.
Lyric Poetry of the Æolians, 17, 18.
   of the Dorians, 18, 19.
Lyrical Parts in Attic Drama, 20–23.

M.
Metre, 37.
Metrical Licenses, 74–76.
Music, 24.
Myurus, 16.

N.
Nævius, 25.
Nonnus, 23.

O.
Ovid, 29, 30.

P.
Pacuvius, 25.
Peculiarities of Prosody in Homer, 111–113.
   in Latin, 114, 115.
Pentameter, 16.
Period, 19, 23, 40.
Phædrus, 26.
Phalæcean Verse, 18, 28.
Pherecratean Verse, 65.

Index. 121

Pindar, 19.
Plautus, 25, 26.
Porfyrius Optatianus, 33.
Position, 108, 109.
Propertius, 30.
Prudentius, 35.
Punctuation, 43-46.
Pythiambic System, 72, 73.

Q.

Quantitative Principle, 13.

R.

Rhyme, 46, 47.
Rhythm, 37.
Rhythmical Poetry, 36.
Rhythmical Structure of the Verse, 77-79.
of the Hexameter and Pentameter, 79-83.
of the Remaining Metres, 83-85.
Rutilius Namatianus, 32.

S.

Sapphic Strophe, 68, 69.
Sapphic Verse of Fifteen Syllables, 66.
Sappho, 17, 18.
Saturnian Verse, 24, 25.
Seneca, 32.
Septimius Serenus, 33.
Simmias, 24.
Simonides, 19.
Sophocles, 21.
Sotadic Verse, 23.

Spondiazon, 51.
Stesichorus, 19.
Stichomythy, 20.
Strophe, 19, 43.
Strophes in Later Times, 32, 34.
Syllable, Last, of the Verse, 42, 43, 48.
Symmetry, 40, 42.
Synaphcia, 42, 43, 48.
Synizesis in Greek, 92.
in Latin, 93-95.
Syrus, 26.
System, 43.

T.

Terence, 25, 26.
Terentianus Maurus, 33.
Thesis, 38.
Resolution of, 48, 49.
Tibullus, 30.
Tmesis, 87, 88.
Tragedy of the Time of Augustus, 31.
Trochaic Metres, 62, 63.

V.

Varro Atacinus, 28.
Varro Reatinus, 29.
Vergil, 29, 30.
Verse, 40, 41.
Verse-feet, 38-40.
Versification, Ancient, in its Development, 13, 14.
Greek, compared with Roman, 14.
Final State of, 34.
Versus Politicus, 36.
Vowels, Successive Sounds, 89-91.

www.ingramcontent.com/pod-product-compliance
Lightning Source LLC
Chambersburg PA
CBHW020124170426
43199CB00009B/632